DISTINCTIVE DISCIPLESHIP

Designing Specific Plans for Christian Maturity

DISTINCTIVE DISCIPLESHIP

Designing Specific Plans for Christian Maturity

TRAVIS AGNEW

DISTINCTIVE DISCIPLESHIP

Tag Publishing

Printed in the United States of America.

Design by Daniel Gibson.

ISBN: 9781086604214

To Robert,

Your writings challenged my thinking,
but your example changed my life.

TABLE OF CONTENTS

PREFACE

Why did I write this book?

1. I wrote this book out of respect to those who asked for it. While we explored how to implement this process within our church, some of you encouraged me to write it down to make it more widely available. Your encouragement served as the needed impetus for this book's completion.

2. I wrote this book within the context of our church family. We unveiled the model, and you jumped right into it. I am amazed at the testimonies I hear from those actively engaging in discipleship. As God continues to send more people our way, I pray this resource will help ground us in a discipleship model with a longer shelf life than a simple seasonal emphasis.

3. I wrote this book among the encouragement of my family. Amanda, Obadiah, Eli, and Gloria, you precious people foster a culture of discipleship in our home that few could imagine. Your joyful eagerness and sincere dedication push me more than you could know.

4. I wrote this book for the one holding it. For whatever reason you have decided to give this content a serious look, I am sincerely grateful. I pray that you would benefit greatly from what God has been teaching me.

5. I wrote this book to help do my part in Jesus' Great Commission. Jesus, you have changed my life, and I will use whatever time I have left to help change the lives of others. You are worth all of this and so much more.

CHAPTER 1
DISCIPLESHIP REORIENTATION

"Go therefore and make disciples of all nations..."
(Matt. 28:19).

Most Christians can easily communicate the importance of making disciples, but few can articulate how they are personally engaging in the process. Proclaiming the need for discipleship in theory is not the same as prioritizing its implementation in life. Most churches and ministries are very busy with numerous activities, yet many regularly lament the lack of tangible success despite extensive efforts.

> **What if the problem is not *what* we are doing, but *how* we are doing it?**

Despite our sincere intentions, we will fail at making many disciples if we are unable to make just one. Our efforts are often unsuccessful simply because they are unfocused. The destination of discipleship is the same for every individual, but each unique journey demands specific directions.

Think of it like you would a Sunday morning. As people gather at a church campus for worship, they all arrived at the same place yet traveled by different paths. Some took a left out of their driveways while others turned right. The commutes of some took less than ten minutes while others required more time. Upon arriving at the destination, some saw the church buildings through the driver's side window, while others viewed them through the passenger's side. The church all gathered to the same place, but none of them shared the identical set of directions to get there. If someone wanted to join you next week, you are unable to give instructions if you don't know where they are starting. It is impossible to provide directions to the destination until you identify the point of origin.

The same is true for our spiritual conditions. While all true Christians will end up in the same place one day, none of us are in the same position currently. We all might be aiming for spiritual growth, but we each are starting from different bases and stunted by unique challenges. All of our advantages, disadvantages, successes, failures, habits, and surprises have positioned each of us at different starting locations. Christian maturity should be the ambition for every single one of us, but none of us are lingering in a precisely similar situation as another in our spiritual development.

That's why our call to make disciples is so important. While our souls are where they need to be after conversion, that does not mean that they are where God wants them to stay. We must grow up in our faith. If the goal of spiritual formation is to see immature believers grow into mature disciple-makers, we must have a coherent strategy. Followers of Jesus do not gradually look more like him by accident. If every Christian is in a spiritually unique place surrounded by specific challenges, why do we think that a broad approach will work for every single one of us? Each of us needs a precise plan whether we realize it or not.

THE NEED FOR SIMPLICITY

While we tout the ideal of simple approaches, we are anything but simple people. Each person requires a distinct amount of intentionality, and we each require ongoing evaluation to determine our needs since we all are constantly changing. Finding a thorough strategy for a church is daunting, but designing a specific plan for each member seems downright infeasible. We need a simple approach for the masses that will allow us to develop a detailed strategy for each individual.

Regardless of the overarching immensity of such a looming call, that ideal is Christ's expectation on his Church. The task of making disciples is a unified command but requiring diverse approaches. Each person is undeniably and remarkably different. We each come from contrasting backgrounds with varying needs. While we all start as infants in Christ, we each come from different environments with certain dispositions surrounded by unique relationships and carrying distinct baggage to which no other person can entirely relate.

Generalized approaches can never fully address distinct disciples.

With the massive task of discipling so many complex people, our efforts inadvertently drift towards ignoring the individual while emphasizing the institution. We often desire to formalize a contextual practice into a universal program, personalize a strategy that worked on one and mandate it upon others, or idealize a utopian scenario at which we will never arrive. We tend to prioritize a program's values over a person's needs.

In our churches, we employ broad approaches for unique individuals. While God does use our vast corporate attempts, we discover within the biblical narrative and within our particular experiences that God moves uniquely with each specific person. What is descriptive in the life of one is not necessarily prescriptive in the lives of all.

God is so intentional that he never utilizes a template that he forces upon each one of us. He is a purposeful Father who knows how to care for every single one of his children. God knows where you are right now, and he also knows the specific step that you need to take next. If God didn't use a cookie-cutter approach when he created us, why then would we use generic efforts to disciple one another now?

Since there are so many needs, we often attempt a one-size-fits-all system. Most of our efforts in churches center around shotgun approaches with sincere hopes of impacting the majority of people. While this well-intended approach is logical reasoning, the process is not accomplishing satisfactory spiritual results.

A sermon is a powerful medium to disperse information, but it is not ideal in the direct oversight of personal application. That is why relying solely on sermon series to fix discipleship problems will never fully succeed. The best curriculum in the world can steadily advance the theological formation of the groups in your church, but they cannot address every need present in every single room. While every believer can benefit from solid teaching on any specific biblical topic at any given time, each person has immediate critical needs that may never be addressed within a church's life cycle of sermons, groups, courses, or events.

The realist in me wants to rely on mass efforts, but the idealist in me cannot escape this truth – our discipleship efforts require distinct approaches. While mass appeals will produce positive trends in discipleship, we will be limited in our success until we discover a way to be intentional with each individual. If that sounds overwhelming, it doesn't have to be. Not only is a Distinctive Discipleship approach imperative, I believe that it is actually possible.

THE GREAT DECOMMISSION

If I informed you that Jesus left a note in your mailbox with critical directions, your schedule would instantaneously simplify. What clarity such a piece of information would bring into your life. The remarkable reality is that Jesus has left us clear marching orders. Your job today is to make disciples. We call his parting words the Great Commission.

> "*All authority in heaven and on earth has been given to me. Go therefore and make disciples of all nations, baptizing them in the name of the Father and of the Son and of the Holy Spirit, teaching them to observe all that I have commanded you. And behold, I am with you always, to the end of the age*" (Matt. 28:18-20).

Typically, someone's last words have a unique impact on his or her loved ones. Those final pieces of communication should hold a lasting effect, especially if you are the Son of God. You would think that the followers of Jesus would take those parting words and base their lives upon them. In some ways, many believers have prioritized Jesus' strategy over the last few centuries, but in other ways, we are still in danger of severe neglect. We are guilty of quoting the Great Commission more often than we have applied it.

- The Great Commission given to all disciples has turned into the Great Suggestion reserved for the serious few.
- The Great Commission intended for obedience has been altered to the Great Omission associated with negligence.
- The Great Commission urging us to make disciples has drifted to the Great Decommission enabling us to make excuses.

Instead of allowing Jesus' words to reorient our purpose on earth, we have practically disregarded it from our everyday lives. While Jesus' clarion call was meant to activate us to this work of discipleship, we have resorted to spectating upon the sidelines. We expect the religious professionals to handle the task given to the Church at large. This decommission is unacceptable! There is a reason why "discipler" isn't an actual word. Being a disciple implies that you should be discipling someone else, as well.

The end result of the Great Commission is explicit. Success will be determined by exponential multiplication rather than just explainable addition. If the primary growth of our churches is due to transferring people from one membership role to another, we are failing. We need conversion growth to increase and transfer growth to decrease.

Some Christians do take evangelism seriously. The positive trends are encouraging, but evangelism is not the complete solution. Much of the problem in the Church today is not that we have an evangelism problem but a discipleship problem. The Spirit causes people to be born again, and somehow we expect spiritual infants to transform into mature disciples overnight without any intentional supervision on our part.

The Great Commission calls us to make disciples - not converts.

As he ascended into the skies, Jesus clarified our purpose of discipleship when he delivered the Great Commission. The job is incomplete when someone comes to faith in Christ. Discipleship – and not conversion – is the goal.

Evangelism is necessary, but it is not ultimate. Even though many of us possess a crippling fear surrounding the task of evangelism, we at least acknowledge that we are supposed to be involved in such work. The danger lies not in focusing upon evangelism but in neglecting discipleship.

So why are we so unwaveringly fixated on the originating moment of faith while neglecting the ongoing development of faith? Birthed out of legitimate concern to see sinners transformed by the gospel and to avoid the fires of hell, many Christians focus on pinpointing a moment of conversion rather than prioritizing a lifetime of progression. Once a person raises a hand, walks an aisle, or says a prayer, we all utter a collective sigh of relief that heaven issued another get-out-of-hell free card before it was too late. For all practical purposes, the colossal burden of another's spiritual condition is alleviated from us as soon as a person initially claims to follow Christ.

The only problem with this line of thinking is that our work is not complete once a person becomes a Christian. The initial step of following Jesus is critical, and no other subsequent steps can be taken without it, but it is not the exclusive expectation. In fact, winning a soul for Christ was never meant to be the solitary goal. The point of conversion is not to escape the devil but to embrace the divine. It is the kindness of God that leads us to repentance (Rom. 2:4) – not the fear of hell. So if our spiritual strategies focus solely on evangelism to the neglect of discipleship, we are doing these immature believers a seismic disservice.

Realistically, we spend most of our efforts on making converts instead of disciples because it is easier to measure. We can graph how many people made a momentary decision, but how do we followup to ensure those people are continuing to make lifelong commitments? We must grow disciples into maturity, but we are often immobilized by our inability to articulate how to do it and our fear of doing it wrong. Uncertainty is understandable, but idleness is intolerable.

The result of our inactivity has produced many immature believers who ought to be far more advanced by now (Heb. 5:12). Our churches have been overrun by spiritual infants caring for one another because many have never matured in their faith. We grieve the lack of spiritual vitality among us, but why should we be shocked if we focus on getting someone to walk across the threshold of salvation but rarely teach them how to walk upon the path of application?

THE MODEL OF DISCIPLESHIP

In its simplest form, "disciple" means "learner." A disciple is a student of someone else. In Jesus' day, "disciple" was not a unique term solely reserved for spiritual contexts. It was used to describe whenever one was learning something from another. In our context, we automatically envision a student learning in some educational setting. While a version of classroom learning did exist during Jesus' time, most education was done "along the way" rather than "in the seat." Disciples matured by immersing themselves in modeling, equipping, and implementing types of environments. You weren't a disciple from afar. You could never accept that designation if you only heard the expert nestled from your seat in the back of the classroom. A disciple became a follower of the mentor and learned all that he could by observing the mentor's life up close.

In Jesus' efforts to disciple the original twelve, he exemplified what he expected them to imitate. Choose a small number of people, and ask them to follow you wholeheartedly for a set time. Empty yourself and give them everything you have. Multiply yourself through those disciples, and then send them out to replicate what you did. The process of discipleship is supremely simple yet intricately involved.

If discipleship is so simple in theory, why aren't we doing it?

1. **Apathy** - An apathetic disposition sidelines many people. Too many worldly concerns have stolen our hearts and quieted our passions (2 Tim. 4:10).
2. **Insecurity** - Some allow insecurity to rob us of discipleship opportunities. Many of us have this

imaginary spiritual qualification line in our minds. We honestly believe once we cross it, we will be ready to make disciples. The only problem is that the line continues to distance itself every time we draw near.

3. **Complexity** - We believe that discipleship has a nature of complexity. Unfortunately, we have put so many hurdles in front of our efforts that we honestly buy into the lie that it is too difficult even to attempt.
4. **Unavailability** - Many of us will never engage in discipleship due to our unavailability. People take time and effort, and we would rather meet with them occasionally than walk beside them throughout life.
5. **Unclarity** - Many of us neglect discipleship due to unclarity. While we talk about its importance, we simply don't know where to begin.

That is where I would like for us to start. Let's remove the excuses and get to work. We have wasted enough time despairing our inabilities; it is time to start embracing our opportunities.

A DISTINCTIVE APPROACH

I am going to provide a paradigm for you to initiate. This process will allow you as a distinct disciple-maker to develop a distinct disciple. You don't need my list of what I think is essential. You need a biblical plan to help you engage in a Distinctive Discipleship approach. I will give you some comprehensive broad strokes, but you will need to color in the specific details.

The goal of this book is to help you design a distinctive plan for discipleship.

You will not be discipled by the end of this book, but you will have a game plan for the next few months of your life to that end.

The immediate goal is progression instead of completion. If you implement this plan, you will have a detailed, personalized guide that will set you up for gradual, spiritual success.

As a disciple of Jesus myself, I longed for something that I couldn't easily uncover in the Bible. I wanted a simple discipleship checklist. Knowing the unclarity in my mind and the minds of those around me, I intently desired to develop a thorough guide that I could work through with another individual. Once we could cross off every item on this expansive list, I could present the individual with a certificate of discipleship, and the job would be complete. My dilemma arose when I realized that my list would probably change through the years as well as differ from everyone else's felt priorities. People from different denominations, backgrounds, and nations could never agree on what such a standard should be.

As I investigated options, I was unsettled by the popular notion that mere curriculum completion guarantees spiritual maturity. Completing a workbook does not equate to arriving at wholeness as a disciple. Many helpful attempts at discipleship employ measurements to determine how mature a person is. While I appreciate the intention of such tools, I am very skeptical of such a concept. In certain processes, once an individual reaches a certain mature status, that person is designated as a disciple as if the job on his or her soul is complete.

The problem I had with these approaches is that maturity is subjective, if not slippery. I know people who could pass a seminary theological exam and would be classified by such assessments as a mature disciple. Still, if you looked at the spiritual quality of his or her life, the practicum part would not fare so well. Many people have a biblical theology but lack a biblical practice. On the other hand, many people portray a godly lifestyle but lack godly knowledge. Such guides are incapable of graphing variability. I am wary of scales that label someone as mature or not when we are all incomplete, inconsistent, and in-progress.

Any measurement of spiritual health is riddled with manmade flaws. As if the different components are not enough to complicate the matter, each of us finds ourselves moving up and down those specific scales in our spiritual development. The lesson I learned last year will most likely require repetition in a few years from now. My certificate of completion does not prevent me from needing remedial courses in the future. And even if I have been successful through the trials up to this point, there are yet more turns along the way, of which I will require further direction. In discipleship, no one has arrived, and no one will ever arrive entirely in this life.

In my dilemma, I sought to create a workable list, but instead, I discovered a flexible paradigm. While I attempted to develop a discipleship strategy, I stumbled across a simple yet thorough example that floored me. I didn't need to come up with a template because one was already there. Nestled within three verses of Scripture, this versatile plan made perfect sense.

The more I studied it, the more convinced I became that a simple, adaptable, and repeatable plan is precisely what I needed. Perhaps, it is what you have been looking for as well. We don't need a reimagining of discipleship; we need a reorientation. Let's get back to the basics of one disciple giving everything away to another. If we rid ourselves of generic approaches and forced expectations, we can start addressing our actual spiritual positions and start seeing notable progress.

Discipleship is the intentional investment of a believer for the instruction and imitation of another disciple.

We have each lived through soaring successes and frustrating failures. Discipleship is the opportunity to utilize those experiences to advance another. Regardless of how much you think you have, would you be willing to give that to someone else?

In the following pages, I want to give you a plan for Distinctive Discipleship. Honestly, it is so simple that I initially resisted putting it into a book. As I taught the process to others, I was encouraged by church members and church leaders to make it available to people outside of our church family. Their rationale was how desperately a unique yet straightforward approach was needed for others as well. Once I realized that I wasn't the only one frustrated with vague criteria, I decided to develop this into different formats so that it could help a motivated believer narrow down the work into a targeted plan. The prayer for this book is that it can articulate the concepts in such a way that you can understand the paradigm fully and implement it simply.

In this model, you can develop a plan for your growth or the growth of another. By employing this simple guide, you will work within six categories to create a guide to disciple your mentee, your family, or your group. After unpacking the process, you will be able to memorize it effortlessly and continue to fill out additional plans to make more disciples throughout the years. You can use this process with a child or an adult. It requires no specialized curriculum to use. Any person in any nation can utilize it because it is not dependent upon a given scenario or specific program. At the end of this process, no certificates will be provided because only Jesus gets that right to hand those out. When we finally see him, we will finally be like him (1 John 3:2). Until that happens, let's continue to make gradual yet beneficial progress.

Before I explain the six categories, let's do a little more unpacking of necessary discipleship elements, then we can be on our way. These concepts are too important to neglect. If you get these biblical ideas nestled tightly in your soul, you will hopefully be set free to do what Christ commanded you to do – make disciples.

CHAPTER 2

PROGRESSIVE SANCTIFICATION

Now may the God of peace himself sanctify you completely, and may your whole spirit and soul and body be kept blameless at the coming of our Lord Jesus Christ (1 Thess. 5:23).

Jesus is in the business of making all things new, which is glorious to realize since we are each in desperate need of an overhaul. All will share the same product of transformation, but the process will be unique based upon the individual. The Spirit has work to do in each one of us, but the type of work varies from individual to individual.

Disciples are never assembled on conveyor belts but instead crafted by intentional workers.

The gospel teaches us that God made a good creation, we made a bad decision, and yet God had a plan for our redemption. Like new automobiles dazzling on the car lot, we were pristine until the moment we drove onto the road. Our sin totaled our lives to an unrepairable state. Disfigured from the original glory we were supposed to display and damaged to the point of functional immobility, our destiny was to join all the other dilapidated vehicles in the junkyard.

Remarkably, the vehicle designer visited the automobile cemetery. While others couldn't see past the cost of repair, he couldn't escape the value of redemption. He purchased the hunks of junk and decided to make them new again. His unwavering desire was to renew both their vitality and functionality.

While the designer paid the steep price for their restoration, he also provided his trusted car shops with mechanics who possessed all the knowledge and resources they would need to do further work. Something odd happened though in many of these shops. With the tremendous demand for work, they decided to speed up the process. They designed a conveyor belt to process the vehicles at a quicker pace.

These mechanics looked at the first car in line and evaluated its specific needs. The initial vehicle needed a new transmission, front headlights, wheel bearings, and a working muffler. They carefully designed machines to address those very issues. The first car went through successfully, and so they began to put the next vehicles on the line to do the same work.

The only problem was that the next vehicle didn't require that exact type of work. It instead needed a new alternator and some back tires. Yet once the machine got going, there was no stopping it. Every car was going to get the same type of treatment. After all that innovative type of thought and effort, only a few vehicles could drive away repaired.

Just like the vehicles in this illustration, each of us demands complete restoration, but none of us require the same steps to get there. In our churches, we attempt to put every single person on the same spiritual conveyor belt, but not everyone needs the same work done. While we were all rightfully classified as spiritually totaled, we need different types of tuneups. Even if we meet the restoration expectations after some considerable work, we still require regular maintenance and diagnostic troubleshooting. With every passing year, further issues need to be addressed to keep the car running. Discipleship will never be entirely effective if we use generalized approaches on people with particular needs. Our lives are too complicated for a conveyor belt – we require intentional mechanics who discover what we specifically need to get going again and work relentlessly until that becomes a reality.

We misrepresent individuality as the enemy of simplicity. Just because the process requires specific work does not imply that it is too complex to undertake. The process is undeniably simple: discover what is most broken within any given individual and get to work in that exact area at this specific time.

Before you disciple someone else or work on your own personal growth, let's unpack the theology of what is transpiring. What is happening when you move from the junkyard to the shop and then back onto the road? Without clarity of these critical issues, you run the subtle yet dangerous risk of working for redemption rather than working from redemption. In our goal of helping others experience Christian maturity, we must realize there is a human and a divine component to what is happening. While discipleship is the earthly side of our efforts, sanctification is the heavenly side of God's work.

At conversion, someone begins his or her discipleship journey. While we often think the job is finished at that moment, the work is honestly just getting started. God does the saving work, but he invites us to play a part in the sanctification work. The profession of faith is necessary for salvation (Rom. 10:9). Failure to do so will cause Jesus to deny you (2 Tim. 2:12; Matt. 7:23). Signaling a profession of faith is vitally important yet incomplete.

If there is a true profession of faith, there should be a true progression of faith.

Believers must progress beyond the initial claims of faith. It validates that conversion actually took place. You are not saved by good works (Eph. 2:9), but you are saved for good works (Eph. 2:10). In the life of a believer, good works reveal that you genuinely have been redeemed. People changed by the gospel don't stay the same. If a person makes a legitimate profession of faith, we should witness a longterm progression of faith.

1 GOAL

The gospel is the good news of the saving work of Jesus Christ. The Holy God created all things and has the sole sovereignty over all things. As created beings, we each rebelled against his authority and attempted positioning ourselves to assume his unparalleled right to define what is good and evil. Due to such insurrection, we were rightfully barred from entering heaven upon death. While we deserved God's judgment, we can receive his mercy through the person of Jesus. By living a perfect life, Jesus was able to do what we could not do. When he went to the cross, he offered an opportunity to exchange places and performances with him. He who knew no sin became sin so that, in him, we might become the righteousness of God (2 Cor. 5:21). Jesus went to the cross with our sin upon his record, and we have been credited with his perfect performance upon our account.

The way of salvation is not proving yourself but trusting in Christ.

Our sin has created an eternal dilemma for each of us. I will trust in myself or Jesus for salvation. You have to make that decision as well. Each of us will attempt to make our way back to God or accept the fact that God made a way to us. The gospel call offers all who hear it this simple choice: trust yourself or trust Jesus?

Jesus could walk on water, and yet I struggle getting from a point of origin to a point of destination without tripping over my own feet. Jesus was able to live 33 years without a trace of sin, and I can barely make it 33 minutes without a sinful disaster of epic proportions. Jesus rose from the dead, and I struggle waking up in the morning to read about it. So who should I trust?

The gospel is good news – we can be saved by grace through faith (Eph. 2:8). Jesus has made a way for us to know him yet again! God demonstrated his love toward us in that while we were still sinners, Christ died for us (Rom. 5:8). Through the righteousness of Jesus, we can walk behind him now and with him forever. Once someone receives that glorious gospel message (John 1:12), he or she should subsequently begin the exhilarating process of discipleship.

2 DANGERS

There is a narrow road of biblical Christianity that Jesus said few will ever walk upon (Matt. 7:14). Upon this road, there are two dangers – one on each side. If not careful, you could fall into either one of these ditches and get yourself into serious spiritual trouble.

The first ditch is called legalism. It's a trap requiring someone to do good works in order to earn God's approval. Wielding a list of religious rules, legalists bar anyone from walking with Jesus until they have cleaned their act up by their own volition. While most legalists start with a conviction for holiness, eventually, they find themselves even more strict than God's Word by supplementing the Bible with additional rules that they hold as equivalent to commandments. As long as you keep all their expectations, you can be accepted. Their message is if you can prove yourself, you can earn God's love. That's not the gospel. That is completely contrary to the gospel.

The second dangerous ditch is the complete opposite side of the road from legalism. So many people and churches despised the pharisaical ditch so much, they actually overcompensated and swerved to the other perilous ditch called easy-believism. It's a trap that makes people think that Jesus loves you so much that you will never have to change. It's a form of cheap grace. This type of faith focuses on God's reception and neglects our repentance.

We live in a time when people are walking around our confused culture, dripping from baptismal waters while lacking legitimate soul transformation. Echoing in their heads, they can hear a pastor affirming, "No matter what happens after this moment, you are going to heaven." Such a careless attempt at momentary assurance can lead to eternal regret. After a raised hand or a baptismal plunge, that person may never hear about the need to grow in faith or progress in obedience. Instead of running from their sin, they get comfortable with it.

Many people who had an emotional experience wrongfully assume they had a spiritual transformation.

Guilt from Saturday night's activities does not necessarily equate to redemption in Sunday morning's services. Some people believe that salvation is attempting to walk away from the consequences of a sinful decision, but instead, it is walking toward communion with the sinless Redeemer. We don't come to Jesus to get out of trouble; we come to Jesus because we want him!

Jesus said that a tree is known by its fruit (Matt. 12:33). Good trees produce good fruit; bad trees produce bad fruit. If the roots go deep, the fruit will spread wide.

You don't have to guarantee a change in order to be saved, but if you are truly saved, you are going to display change eventually. It will happen! You don't have to obey Jesus before you are loved by him (legalism), but his love for you should motivate your obedience to him. Salvation doesn't give you a free pass to indulge (easy-believism), but it provides you an eager desire to obey. If there is a true profession of faith, there will be a true progression of faith.

3 COMPONENTS

To grasp the theology of what is happening in the process of discipleship, you must understand the difference between these three theological terms:

1. **Justification** - the declaration of holiness
2. **Sanctification** - the process of holiness
3. **Glorification** - the completion of holiness

Justification is the moment when you are declared not guilty. As God presides over eternity's courthouse, there was a moment when your name was called to appear before the stand. The overwhelming evidence demanded a decisive verdict. You had been caught repeatedly in sin, and your rebellion was unashamedly defiant. Upon hearing the gospel of Jesus, you trusted in his role as your substitute and were forever changed. You were converted. You were reborn.

At that moment, the gavel falls in the courtroom, and you are justified because Christ was willing to pay the sentencing for you. That means that the charges are no longer attributed to you, and Jesus has paid the penalty in full. At the moment you receive the gospel, God justifies you, and that status can never be changed since you are safely secure within his hands (John 10:28).

When justification transpires, God declares you holy. Your scandalous rap sheet has been dealt with, and you exit out of the courtroom without a trace of sin. Justification is a very, very good day.

If justification is the declaration of holiness, glorification is the completion of holiness. When you receive the gospel, you are declared holy. When you reach heaven, you are wholly holy. No percentages of holiness are allowed there. There is no more room or need to make progress. You are finally holy. You are forever glorified on that unthinkable day when you behold Jesus face to face.

The God who justified us will also glorify us (Rom. 8:30). Whether Christ comes back within my lifetime or I die to before that end, I will soon behold Jesus and be with him in glory (Col. 3:4). In that splendid instance, the veil comes off, and we can see the grandeur of the Lord fully (2 Cor. 3:18). At the realization of my heavenly citizenship, he will transform my lowly body into a glorious body like his (Phil. 3:20-21). All of the harmful, sinful things of earth will forever be barred from the gates of heaven (Rev. 21:4).

Glorification is the day when we meet Jesus face to face and don't have to worry about sin anymore. We go to heaven and are perfect. With eternity to enjoy, we say good riddance to the unholiness of our lives and that which is present in this current world. Glorification is a very, very good day.

Justification makes my record non-guilty. Glorification finally obtains that reality. While I was legally declared holy on that day of justification, I will be realized as holy on that day of glorification.

1. Justification is entirely the work of God.
2. Glorification is entirely the work of God.
3. Sanctification is entirely the work of God **and** us.

It would make sense that the one spiritual element that doesn't happen successfully in a solitary moment would be the one in which we get some of the credit. Christians love talking about the day when we met Jesus or when we will see Jesus, but what about every other critical day when we are supposed to become like Jesus? Even our worship includes justification songs and glorification songs, but rarely do we sing about the sanctifying and struggling days in between. Yet these days are critical to the process that God is doing in our lives. We cannot abandon sanctification just because it is difficult.

> **We remember justification, we anticipate glorification, but we are neglecting sanctification.**

Sanctification represents every critical day in between believing the gospel and beholding the Savior. It is the process of holiness that is continually worked on from the day of conversion until the moment of completion. This critical period is the time of discipleship.

- From a **heavenly** perspective, **sanctification** is God's process of making you more holy.
- From an **earthly** perspective, **discipleship** is our effort in the process of becoming more holy.

While justification and sanctification are entirely the work of the Lord, sanctification is the work of the Lord and us. Sanctification is hard work, and it will not be complete until we die. Notice that I didn't say it happens once we die but that we complete it once we die. After our profession of faith, we should spend the remainder of our life in the glorious pursuit of spiritual progression.

The proof that we are neglecting sanctification is the lack of holiness present in so many Christians. For many of us who claim to follow Jesus, we aren't that close in proximity to him. An honest review over the last few years would reveal how much progress you have actually made. Sure, you will have moments of failures along the way, but are you trending towards more holiness or complacently settled into further unholiness?

We cannot blame this lack of sanctification on inability but neglect. God would not call you to a task in which he would not provide you the tools. If we aren't gravitating towards further development, it is because we don't prioritize discipleship enough. Each of us progresses in that which we prioritize. We put the utmost efforts into workout regimens, home renovation, graduate degrees, extracurricular activities, and any glittering pursuit that this world provides. People know how to put in work, but are we working on the most important things?

> *If you put these things before the brothers, you will be a good servant of Christ Jesus, being trained in the words of the faith and of the good doctrine that you have followed. Have nothing to do with irreverent, silly myths. Rather train yourself for godliness; for while bodily training is of some value, godliness is of value in every way, as it holds promise for the present life and also for the life to come. The saying is trustworthy and deserving of full acceptance. For to this end we toil and strive, because we have our hope set on the living God, who is the Savior of all people, especially of those who believe* (1 Tim. 4:6-10).

While you thank God for justification and wait for glorification, you should be partnering with him for yours and others' sanctification. Like Paul instructed Timothy, are you presently toiling and striving towards this end? While there is plenty of training that provides value, we must prioritize training ourselves for godliness, which provides the most significant benefit. Without a doubt, God is committed to that end, but sometimes we are lagging in our personal responsibility.

In the verses above, Paul gave a great example to his disciple, Timothy. He raised many questions for us to consider:

1. How devoted are you to study the task at hand?
2. Are you sitting under those you would consider experts and learning from them?

3. How active are you fighting against the sin areas in your life?

4. Can you see an improvement in your level of Kingdom activity?

5. Are you pouring out what you are learning into another?

6. Do you have a yearning to know Jesus more than you do right now?

7. Does your schedule reflect that your sanctification is a priority?

We are saved by grace, and that grace changes us to do good works. When we become saved, we experience justification (we are seen as guiltless in the eyes of the Judge). When we go to heaven, we experience glorification (we don't sin anymore). The middle process of sanctification is laborious and often neglected. It reminds us that we won't be perfect until we get to heaven, but we should be getting there. Progress should be evident. We need to be improving. Throughout our lives, there should be some evidence of our growth to becoming more like Jesus.

THE STARTING LINE

If we are to accept Christ's discipleship call, we must embrace the entirety of his process, and that includes intentional investment into our spiritual conditions. Instead of allowing that to discourage you, be encouraged that God Almighty isn't through with you yet (Phil. 1:6), and he is wholly committed to seeing you through it all (Eph. 2:10). Could you ask for anyone more qualified to be in your corner?

As people who have been saved by the gospel of Jesus, we are meant to go with the gospel of Jesus. When God provides the opportunities to proclaim truth to another, it is phenomenal to see when he uses those imperfect efforts to transform lives. Sharing the good news will lead others to legitimate saving faith, but the job is not complete at that time. While we rejoice in those moments, we don't rest after those moments.

Salvation is the starting line – not the finishing line.

Once a person is saved by grace through faith (Eph. 2:8), the journey is just getting started. It is not merely time to shift focus on to another evangelism prospect when the previous one is no longer endangered by eternal punishment. If we really prioritized evangelism, we would disciple each new convert so that our evangelistic efforts would experience multiplication rather than just mere addition. We must do more than convincing converts; we must develop disciples. In reality, many Christians fail to do the task of evangelism because they were never truly discipled. If we want our evangelism to increase, we must address our discipleship. It is difficult to give something away you don't possess yourself.

Before making disciples of all nations, we better start by attempting to make at least one. It is time to get acquainted with the starting line. Are you ready to take this Great Commission seriously and personally? Regardless of your fears, I promise you that you can make a disciple. I never promised that you could earn a theological degree, hone a teaching mastery, or memorize a curriculum, but I do believe that you can use your life for discipleship purposes. For you to make a disciple successfully, we have to get back to the simple yet distinct approach. Now that we understand the theology of how it happens, we must address a critical point of methodology to ensure it happens. Many people never progress any further in their sanctification due to lacking one specific element.

CHAPTER 3

INTENTIONAL IMITATION

Be imitators of me, as I am of Christ (1 Cor. 11:1).

We have highlighted the need for discipleship and unpacked the nature of discipleship, but it is now time to address one of the most glaringly obvious omissions in our discipleship – the person doing the discipling. While that component seems apparent, it increasingly is not. Our commitment to fleshing out our personal walks with Christ overlooks our need to learn from one another.

True discipleship prioritizes imitation over information.

Our shelves and devices are full of opportunities to increase our learning. We have more biblical information now than ever before, but we are desperately missing biblical transformation. I am not making a case that knowledge is irrelevant. We need to develop a biblical understanding more than ever, but how do we expect to learn the content to the fullest degree without some example in front of us? Authentic disciples first possess the Word of God and the Spirit of God to direct them, but both of those point to our need to learn from others.

By our efforts, you would discern that we think the acquisition of quality content is the key to our growth. If we collect enough knowledge, we will reach the desired destination. That's why we focus on leadership personalities over leadership proximities. We resort to learning from the expert from afar rather than watching a mentor up close.

I believe our churches need to grow, but with any growth comes additional complexities with which we must consider. The goal is not to halt numerical growth but to ensure spiritual growth along the way. With more people, the nature of connection grows ever more complicated. The larger we fill our worship auditoriums with people continues to distance members from their pastors. The more video-based our Bible study curriculum continues to be, the more we rely upon the unknown expert rather than learning from the untapped person pressing play in the room. The more often we emphasize resources over relationships proves that we don't think we need each other. Each of us requires someone a little further ahead on the journey to point us in the right direction.

We each have distinct needs, and we each need a distinct guide.

How would you answer this question – have you been discipled? Most people give a complex answer to that simple question. Apparently, the answer is yes and no for many of us. You have been discipled to some extent, but few of us have ever experienced the level of intentionality that we see in Scripture. Discipleship is taking everything you know about Jesus and passing it on to another. Has anyone ever done that for you? Have you ever done that for someone?

In every new generation of Christians, we tend to criticize the failures of those before us. Faulting the discipleship efforts of previous generations is an unhelpful tactic when you simply point out their shortcomings without providing any solutions. The people in the past may be easy targets, but analyzing them doesn't get us any closer to the goal. Just because you are a critic of yesterday's church does not make you an expert of today's church. If we spent half the time that we have used denouncing how others haven't discipled people and used it to disciple others, we would start fixing our problem.

It is an easy approach to grow a church by demeaning other churches. The problem in our discipleship isn't as simple as an outdated worship style, formal type of classroom, or stuffy religious buildings. If we genuinely investigate the situation, the church of the past must have done something right to produce such knowledgable critics as ourselves. I grew up in church and now serve as a pastor. My story is contingent upon yesterday's church because they introduced me to Jesus, baptized me, discipled me, counseled me, equipped me in seminary, sent me on missions, and so much more. Anyone can point out holes in a system, but a grateful leader shouldn't waste time masking insecurities by criticizing others.

The church of the past may not have done everything right, but they got something right.

Most likely, I won't get everything right either. Instead of focusing on what was broken in the past, why not look at what we can do better in the present? In recent decades, many churches have advanced at getting quality information out there. I see significant improvements along the way to update methods without abandoning the message. As I look at the current state of churches today, I think one way we can improve is by focusing on nurturing relationships within the church. It is imperative that what we teach is reliable, but we are working to our disadvantage if we are not emphasizing those mature teachers among us.

The church of the recent past did a great job talking about the need for discipleship, but many struggled with setting up the environments needed for discipleship. While some level of discipleship does happen in the context of a full worship service with a biblical preacher and in the safety of a vibrant room of people committed to in-depth Bible study, it will never reach its full potential until it gets to a life-on-life model. I think many churches have the content down pat but are neglecting the medium through which the material is best transferred.

Have you been discipled? If you have been a part of a local church, I would affirm that you have been to some degree. By receiving biblical instruction and experiencing opportunities for spiritual growth, I would venture to say you have been developed. Have you been thoroughly discipled? Unless you have ever had a person say to you, "Come, follow me," I am going to assume that a vital element in your story is missing.

6 COMMON COMPONENTS

Personal testimonies are encouraging stories to hear. Learning how God uniquely changed a life reminds us of his intentionality and creativity. No story is the same. While testimonials of how people grow are different, common components emerge in almost every account. The more stories you hear, the more you might notice similar items. What about your testimony? If you took the time to archive your discipleship journey thus far, you would probably be amazed at all the waypoints along the path.

This process would be helpful for you at this point. I would encourage you to take a few moments and think through your story. Don't write a narrative, but jot down some bullet points of the most critical elements that have contributed to your growth thus far. Write them either in the space below or in a journal:

Now that you have taken a trip down your spiritual memory lane, I want to help you designate each significant component. In the stories of growing disciples, I often find these six common components: event, environment, example, encourager, equipment, and engagement. Let me unpack them, and then I want you to discover how many are tucked within your story.

1. **Event** - Do you have a milestone when God changed your life? In most stories, there is a defining moment or defining moments that changed everything for an individual. The pivotal event might have been during that service when the gospel finally came alive inside you. Maybe it was that quiet time in that beautiful location where God made something abundantly clear. It could have been when tragedy hit your life, and you had to rely on God like never before. Whether a positive or a negative event, those events often serve as catalysts for spiritual growth.

2. **Environment** - What regular faith gatherings shaped who you are today? While the event mentioned previously might have been a single occurrence, the environment component served more as a consistent greenhouse for some season in your life. These regular faith gatherings helped shape your faith leanings. Maybe the environment that changed you was that regular worship attendance, small group study, or parachurch ministry gathering. The consistent pattern of meeting together provided a structure of growth for you. The connections in those pivotal services or studies made a lasting impact.

3. **Equipment** - What spiritual disciplines trained you to grow in godliness? Every person who is genuinely advancing in faith has some habit they picked up along the way that increased their commitment. While the

discipline will vary from person to person, most of us can testify to some specialized equipment that was initialized and utilized during an essential time of rapid growth. Standard pieces of equipment in the life of a disciple are regular Bible reading, vibrant prayer habits, or generous giving trends. When a particular discipline becomes a passionate habit, significant growth occurs in the life of the disciple.

4. **Engagement** - How did you intentionally invest in another with what you learned? For most disciples, a moment occurred when they stopped receiving and started giving. The engagement might have been realized on a mission trip or through ministry service, but it pinpoints a way you started giving feet to your commitment. The process of putting your faith into practice can jumpstart the discipleship process. When a disciple begins to engage in the mission and give one's life away, rapid growth is always a byproduct.

5. **Encourager** - Who is that friend or friends who walked beside you and pushed you towards Christ? Most growing disciples had people spurring them on during critical junctures of their lives. These encouragers were pivotal because they provided encouragement and accountability. Once these relationships were realized, you understood that you were not on your own, and, most likely, you went further faster.

6. **Example** - Who is the example you aspired to follow? While the encourager walked beside you, this example walked ahead of you. This person displayed a rare personification of living for Jesus that seemed mesmerizingly contagious to you. Whether intentional or unintentional, oftentimes, you found a mentor that

inspired you. Some individual cast a shadow over your life that caused you to pursue everything differently.

How many of those six components are present in your story? I would recommend taking a moment and going back to your story page and designating where you see these six items. Just place the name or number beside each point you made and see what you have experienced up to this point in your life.

When I have done this exercise with people, most people easily identify five out of the six. The example is the glaringly missing component in most spiritual stories. Many people will say they had a parent, pastor, mentor, or leader that impacted them, but only a few felt like it was an intentional process of discipleship.

Christians often feel that their mentoring happened by default rather than by design.

Each of us has systematically learned from others, but you may have never been intentionally mentored by another. We need an intentional mentor in our lives, and we need to be that for someone else. Just consider the bold assertion of 1 Cor. 11:1: “Be imitators of me, as I am of Christ.” If anyone other than the Apostle Paul said that to you, you would consider him or her to be an oblivious braggart. The audacity to walk up to another believer and instruct him or her that the secret to Christian living is imitating you seems ludicrous, but it is the essential element needed. Paul tells this church if they want to imitate Jesus, they should imitate him. Since he is imitating Jesus to the best of his ability, his example should put them in that proper place as well. Regardless of how prideful it might sound to our self-deprecating ears, it is the biblical example for us to follow. Discipleship is often caught more than taught, and we need people in our lives from whom we can learn how to follow Jesus.

While Timothy had encouragers in his life (Acts 16:2), he needed the example in the Apostle Paul (Acts 16:3; 2 Tim. 1:13). Moses had experienced the life-changing event of the parting of the Red Sea (Ex. 14:21); however, he still desperately needed the intentionality of the seasoned Jethro to show him how to lead these newly freed people (Ex. 18:19). Samuel was busy ministering in the name of the LORD (1 Sam. 3:1), but he needed Eli to teach him how to discern the voice of the LORD (1 Sam. 3:9).

One thing you don't notice in the New Testament is a potential disciple asking to follow the mentor. When someone does ask to follow Jesus, he replies with a poignant question to hear the level of commitment. Regarding the disciples who started and finished with Jesus, he was always the initiator. The teacher approached the prospective students and invited them to an adventure like none other. Whether it was the fishermen in the boat (Matt. 4:18-22), the tax collector at the financial booth (Matt. 9:9), or the skeptic studying under the tree (John 1:46-48), Jesus started the conversation in their place of contextual comfort. These men were not begging to follow Jesus; he intentionally invited them to come along. Even after his resurrection, we still read of Jesus approaching them to communicate further instructions (Matt. 28:18).

I share this point to highlight a severe deficiency in our discipleship process: mentees are seeking mentors, yet mentors are often not seeking mentees. Most would claim that it seems awkward to assume you have something to offer another, but that is what we sorely need. Every disciple would benefit from an intentional mentor providing an example worth imitating.

Generation after generation is attempting to navigate life without insight from those who have gone before them. As the family continues to distance itself from one another and hesitant mentors shortchange their ability to influence another for good, numerous people are drifting confused and chaotic. No one ever posted the detour signs along life's journeys, and so people continually contribute to the wreckage on the side of the road.

For all the shortcuts learned along the way, they are often never shared with those coming behind. Our negligence invites others to repeat our mistakes and remain ignorant of our guidance.

ONE SIZE FITS ONE

I never trust the "one size fits all" label on clothing, and I definitely disregard it when it comes to spiritual matters. With all of our unique challenges, we need a distinctive plan and an intentional guide. Is it possible to have a general goal of discipleship yet a specific direction for each individual?

Jesus apparently did. In addition to the numerous people Jesus impacted during his time on earth, he intentionally discipled twelve men. Over three years, these men accompanied him almost every waking hour. While Jesus gave sermons and examples to the masses, he apparently was also working towards particular ends with each disciple.

Take Peter, for example. During Jesus' ministry, Peter struggled the most when suffering was possible. Peter confessed Jesus as the Christ until the Christ talked about a cross (Matt. 16:21-23). He was ready to pull out the sword and go to arms against his enemies before ever succumbing to surrender and joining Jesus in imprisonment or suffering (John 18:10). Confronted by a harmless girl, he began to swear his disassociation with Jesus to keep himself secure (Matt. 26:69-75). How can we not recognize that by the time Jesus has worked on him, he remarkably counts suffering as honorable (Acts 5:27-32) and writes a letter where suffering is the unifying theme (1 Pet. 2:21)?

For John, it wasn't suffering, but the distinctive issue appeared to be a need for him to grow in his love for others. They called him a Son of Thunder for a reason (Mark 3:17). He got upset when outsiders seemed successful (Mark 9:38). It is challenging to be zealous for God's work when you are jealous of who gets the credit. When he encountered unreceptive people, he was eager to attempt calling fire down from heaven to consume such unthinkable unbelievers (Luke 9:54). For all his brazen behavior, something changed inside him along the way. Would Jesus entrust his aging mother to an unstable hothead (John 19:26-27)? John began to exhibit a tender shepherd's love and encouraged others to follow him in compassionate living (1 John 4:7-8).

Jesus even had a strategy for Thomas. This doubting disciple was often confused regarding the direction of Jesus (John 11:16; 14:5). He initially didn't have the faith needed to see the larger picture. It is undeniably revealing that at the exact moment when Jesus decided to disclose his resurrected self to the disciples, Thomas was the only one absent (John 20:24). If Jesus defeated death and could enter any room with the doors locked, don't you think he was aware that Thomas was missing when he decided to reunite with the group? I do not believe that Thomas' absence caught him by surprise. These disciples were rarely leaving each other due to fear (John 20:19), and yet it just so happens that Jesus waits for Thomas to leave before appearing. What was the motive behind such timing? He was developing Thomas' most distinct need – the increase of his faith (John 20:27-29).

One size doesn't fit all; one size fits one. Jesus knew that. He practiced it. He was developing the entire ragtag group of disciples, but he was employing distinctive approaches with each one. Jesus worked on Peter's steadfastness, John's love, and Thomas' faith, to name a few. He knew them well enough to understand what was lacking at that time and what would be necessary for the future.

THE MISSING COMPONENT

For all the sermons you have heard, for all the studies you have completed, for all the events you have attended, for all the books you have read, and for all the lessons you have learned, you are desperately in need of someone a little further along than you to show you the way. The missing component in most of our spiritual stories is an intentional mentor who values imitation even more than information. Through a consistent example, the content is retained far better than if it just came through a mere resource. No matter how substantial this volume is in your hand, it would have a more meaningful impact if I could flesh these concepts out right beside you.

As you have read this book so far, you might have grown more eager to grow in personal sanctification. With your enthusiasm increasing, the call to have a mentor beside you might be very discouraging. Due to your comfort with the concept or the actual potential of a possible mentor approaching you, this process may have just grown more frustratingly complex. In the next chapter, I will lay out the specifics of how to begin your Distinctive Discipleship plan. As you read it, you may see how you can adapt the concepts and start all by your lonesome. While that is not ideal, any plan is better than no plan. Narrowing down a targeted guide to address your spiritual condition right now is better than just hoping you somehow make progress along the way.

> **While creating a specific plan is good for an individual, it is better with a partner, but best with a mentor.**

I would prefer you to design a plan rather than just aimlessly wandering through religious practices, even if it meant you did it in isolation. Configuring a specific guide is better than doing nothing, but I know that we miss so much of what God intends when we seek to follow Jesus alone without traveling companions. If this resource gives you some goals, that is a great start. I would recommend at least having an accountability partner to know where you are and where you are hoping to go. The sideways collaboration and accountability will serve you well on days that you will struggle to maintain your commitments. Just sharing your plan with another will cause it to be reliably more successful.

A partner beside will benefit you, but a mentor ahead will advance you. You won't find a perfect mentor, but that's kind of the point anyway. The intentional example in front of you will help you align with their effective practices and avoid their unfortunate mistakes. This directive goes both ways. In all the talk of mentoring, you need someone in front of you and someone behind you. Who is discipling you, and who are you discipling?

God has sent many guides in my life. From motivational ministers to faithful friends, I have learned so much from so many different people. While I have gained insight from many, it has been rare in my experience for someone to position his or her life intentionally close enough for me to imitate. Paul saw the same great need in the church at Corinth.

> *For though you have countless guides in Christ, you do not have many fathers. For I became your father in Christ Jesus through the gospel* (1 Cor. 4:15).

What a statement. How many of us could attest to that reality? We have had countless guides but few fathers. Every child in the faith needs a father or mother figure relentlessly investing in him or her. You may not have had that yourself, but will you provide it for another? If someone replicated your spiritual devotion right now, would that be a worthy pursuit?

To find a mentor or a mentee, don't attempt to force a relationship. Seek those who you are naturally around, and pursue a higher level of intentionality with that person. You can grow on your own or alongside a friend, but you will forever be changed by being on either side of an intentional discipling relationship.

CHAPTER 4
STRATEGIC FORMATION

Him we proclaim, warning everyone and teaching everyone with all wisdom, that we may present everyone mature in Christ (Col. 1:28).

It's time to get distinctively practical. If you feel like you are stuck in your Christian walk, then it is time to start moving again. After addressing discipleship reorientation, progressive sanctification, and intentional imitation, it is now time to design a plan for strategic formation. By investigating these essential big-picture issues, it is now necessary to develop a workable plan in which you can disciple another or embark on the next stage of your own discipleship journey. No more happenstance growth, we must be intentional. Let your spiritually frustrated fatigue launch you out of complacency and into maturity.

**It's OK to feel stagnate,
but it's unacceptable to stay that way.**

I know what it is like to feel stuck spiritually. At many times in my life, I have unfortunately felt unsuccessful and unmotivated. Listening to others share regarding their current growth would be more discouraging than encouraging because it provoked an internal concern regarding what was wrong with me. As I beheld their dedication, I feared that my current state was the new normal.

Have you ever felt that way? One of the most sinking realizations is to acknowledge a time in the past when you felt closer to God than you do in the present. If you remember a time when you were more engaged to worship, eager to study, or excited to serve than you are now, it might indicate that you are experiencing a dangerous case of spiritual stagnation. Instead of allowing that to immobilize you, let the present tension propel you to action. If you feel disappointed with your current level of devotion, you can probably guarantee that God would agree with you. The good news is that he is eager to alleviate the distance and prepared to provide a guide.

If you aren't spiritually where you want to be right now, you are in good company. Despite your situation, don't believe the lie that the reason you are struggling is due to a condition you cannot help.

1. If you cannot maintain an authentic passion for worshipping God, it might not be a lack of commitment but a discipleship issue.

2. If you consistently struggle with the same sin area, it might not be a condition problem but a discipleship issue.

3. If you are ignorant concerning a biblical doctrine, it might not be an intelligence deficiency but a discipleship issue.

4. If you believe yourself unqualified to perform a ministry task, it might not be a skill problem but a discipleship issue.

5. If you feel guilty because of your sparse devotional rituals, it might not be a time problem but a discipleship issue.

6. If you sense your prayers lack a level of faith, it might not be a circumstance problem but a discipleship issue.

Are you starting to see a pattern? I am sure your struggles are plausible – I just don't believe them to be paralyzing. If God has called you to develop as a disciple, I cannot envision he would permit anything to render an eager soul helpless to advance in the things that matter most.

The Christian life should be marked by gradual yet continual progress.

If you are tired of settling into a stagnate place, let's start moving again. As mentioned earlier, I grew frustrated with the lack of direction for my personal growth and the absence of a guide to help others grow. I desperately desired to discover a specific checklist by which to make disciples. Impeded by the lack of such a detailed list, I planned to create my own framework but fearful that some critical components would be overlooked.

While my exasperation intensified with being unable to make a thorough plan, I decided to preach through the Book of Colossians at our church. The main reason I wanted to study that particular letter was due to specific content at the end of chapter one. Paul's expressed goal of Christian maturity for these believers was critical for our church to understand. I desired to teach how discipleship would look at the time of our completion.

Paul wrote that the goal of discipleship is to present one another as fully mature in Christ (Col. 1:28). As I read the passage, I symbolically envisioned Paul approaching Christ with his disciples surrounding him. "Jesus, I did everything I could with these people you entrusted me. I taught them absolutely everything I know. I showed them essentially everything I could do. I took them as far as I could take them, and by my estimation, they are fully mature."

Paul's discipleship strategy set out to "present everyone mature in Christ" (Col. 1:28). What a simple yet daunting goal! In assessing an individual, Paul would see what areas needed to be addressed, and then he would get to work. With each disciple, he would find maturity in some areas and immaturity in others. By identifying the critical issues, he could formulate a specific plan.

As the week to preach that passage arrived, I found myself surprised to discover that my desired "discipleship checklist" had been right in front of my eyes all along. In the early morning hours, I found a different type of list than I expected. Instead of specific items, I saw six categories within Paul's writings with which to disciple another.

> *To them God chose to make known how great among the Gentiles are the riches of the glory of this mystery, which is Christ in you, the hope of glory. Him we proclaim, warning everyone and teaching everyone with all wisdom, that we may present everyone mature in Christ. For this I toil, struggling with all his energy that he powerfully works within me* (Col. 1:27-29).

Paul was enraptured by the reality that Christ lived in him. As a result of that marvelous truth, everything had changed. The message of Jesus would define his life and determine his lifestyle. His call for this church provides an excellent framework with which to disciple another. Through the broad strokes provided in the Scriptures, an individual could design a specific plan for Christian maturity around these six areas:

1. **Delight** - "Christ in you, the hope of glory"
2. **Disobedience** - "warning everyone"
3. **Doctrine** - "teaching everyone with all wisdom"
4. **Development** - "present everyone mature in Christ"

5. **Discipline** - "for this I toil"
6. **Dependence** - "struggling with all his energy"

THE 6 CATEGORIES

Paul's description provided this church with six unique discipleship categories. Including negative things to avoid and positive things to embrace, the list proposes sweeping principles with which each person can apply differently. While the following chapters will go deeper into each category concerning how to design a specific plan for each unique person, let me briefly show you how each of these will flesh out. The Distinctive Discipleship model uses a biblical framework to address these specific areas:

1. A disciple must possess an endearing **delight** at the opportunity to follow Jesus. The riches of the glory of this mystery is that the fullness of God dwelt in Christ (Col. 1:19) and that the fullness of Christ dwells in us (Col. 1:27). The delight category focuses on the motivation for discipleship. Are you currently following Jesus out of duty or delight? If your motive for growth is anything other than the delight of knowing Jesus, you will eventually stall out. You don't have to follow Jesus; you get to follow Jesus! This first component seeks to weed out any competing joys that attempt to rival our affection for Jesus.

2. A disciple must commit to warring against any **disobedience** in his or her life. The task of warning everyone (Col. 1:28) implies a commitment to a radical confrontation of sin. Discipleship must alert against disobedience in any sinful leanings specific to the person. Each of us is prone to wander, but we each

wander in different directions. What is the most serious sinful area that must be addressed right now?

3. A disciple must commit to studying a biblical **doctrine** thoroughly. Paul's instruction to teach everyone with all wisdom (Col. 1:28) implies a need to possess a gradually fuller understanding of the whole counsel of God (Acts 20:27). Discipleship must wisely equip the follower to acquire competent biblical doctrine. While we all could know more, what is important to address now? More than a curious topic, what is a critical belief that must be grounded in your mind? Given the specific situation of an individual, what key doctrinal area needs to be strengthened first?

4. Discipleship must address areas of calling with the intention to bring about ministry **development**. If the task is to present everyone mature in Christ (Col. 1:28), we must get to work on the immature areas and not ignore them. By assessing the individual, we determine what needs to be improved in order to present that person as complete in Christ when that day of presentation comes. Considering the gifting of the person and the context of his or her life, what needs to be developed to further ministry work?

5. Discipleship must train in areas of spiritual **discipline** for continual growth. As Paul sought to disciple others, he characterized his efforts as that for which he toiled (Col. 1:29). It was hard work. Every person you would label as mature has applied effort in the spiritual gym by building muscles in those areas that develop one's faith. While there are plenty of things that all of us could improve, what is the most pivotal discipline that would further a disciple on the

journey right now? Which spiritual discipline must be strengthened in order to grow?

6. Discipleship must continually acknowledge the complete **dependence** upon Jesus for the believer's maturity. While Paul admittedly toiled in his efforts, he also realized that he was "struggling with all his energy that he powerfully works within me" (Col. 1:29). As delight in Jesus is the essential beginning for discipleship, a dependence upon Jesus is the necessary conclusion. Any effort made must be understood as utterly dependent upon God's work within us. What are we praying for God to do in the heart of the disciple? How are we longing to see God work in the disciple's life?

Using these six categories, narrow down a timely and targeted Distinctive Discipleship plan that is as unique as the individual.

That's the guide. It can be as simple yet as thorough as you desire to make it. Find a person to disciple and investigate his or her current spiritual condition. As you discover where the person is, you can determine where he or she needs to go next. By using these categories, design a specific plan for a unique person by addressing the areas of delight, disobedience, doctrine, development, discipline, and dependence. While highlighting these particular areas and agreeing upon an initial time of commitment, you can use these broad strokes and develop a Distinctive Discipleship plan by yourself or with another.

Instead of a manmade list, this guide operates from a biblical example. As Paul continued to invest in the Colossian church, he wanted them to maintain the delight of the indwelling Christ, fight against the disobedience threatening their holiness, embolden the doctrine constituting biblical theology, plan for the development of each individual, toil with the disciplines for the purpose of godliness, and prioritize the dependence upon Jesus' power even among their efforts. While these elements were critical for the discipleship of the Colossian church, they prove relevant to us today as well.

Within the subsequent chapters, we will look at how to use each category to develop a detailed approach for a specific person. In reality, the simplicity of the summarized version above could get you started, but the following chapters will provide a comprehensive tool to ascertain clear next steps. After studying this system, it should hopefully serve you well to get started with an adaptable, manageable, memorizable, and repeatable plan.

PRINCIPLES VS. PROGRAMS

Sharing this simple framework is a delicate balance. As I have explained the concepts and utilized them with others, it is straightforward enough that a plan could be drawn out on a napkin. Others encouraged me to flesh out the ideas a little more so that it could be a lasting template to be used in varying contexts.

The hesitation in explaining this content too much is due to a fear that this biblical example could become overly programmatic. This guide is meant to allow you to get started in discipleship without dictating every single step. The Distinctive Discipleship process is a plan but not the only plan. I do believe it can help those who feel stuck. It possesses the type of direction I was praying for but avoids the opportunity to micromanage the process, which often suffocates our efforts.

My prayer is that this content will be principle-based rather than program-driven. Within the broad structure, you can maintain flexibility and adaptability to your contextual process. Here is why I think making this Distinctive Discipleship model a natural part of your life will further your efforts.

1. **Broad Guide** - If you are helplessly tied to a strict curriculum, that process can feel regimented rather than relational. Utilizing this simple approach, you can use this book or a simple scratch piece of paper to get started. The categories will provide the structure, but the actual plan will be as distinct as you and the one you disciple desire it to be.

2. **Adaptable Format** - The simplistic nature of this model allows you to use it in many different variations. A pastor could use it to disciple a minister in training, a group leader could use it on a group member, or a parent could use it for his or her children. You can make it as straightforward or as complex as needed.

3. **Contextual Usage** - This type of format doesn't require you to change a program in your church or drop a curriculum in your rotation. Use your existing programs and relationships to design specific plans. Without having to alter any significant processes, you should be able to use this as a guide to get intentional among previously existing relationships.

4. **Specific Plan** - Instead of sending another person down a ministry conveyor belt, you can get intensely specific about the needs of each individual. Using these categories, you can create a particular list of items to tackle and know how to gauge effectiveness. With this approach, no two plans will be the same.

5. **Timed Commitment** - Without a specific deadline, intentions will wane over time. As you begin this process, I recommend putting an initial timeline together. This step ensures that a process is

put in place to have a target of completion but also an agreed-upon end date if a mentoring relationship doesn't connect naturally. If you design a plan by yourself, this effort still provides an end goal for you to articulate clearly.

6. **Balanced Emphasis** - If left to our leanings, many of us will focus on certain spiritual formation elements to the detriment of others. I have been a member of accountability groups that spent the entirety of our time together bemoaning our sin struggles but failed to address needed biblical clarity. I have also had relationships that prioritized doctrinal discussions and neglected pious progressions. With these six categories, you can make sure your emphasis is comprehensive and balanced to address the whole person.

7. **Unique Contributions** - While each plan will be distinct to the disciple, it will also be distinct to the disciple-maker. If you were discipled by someone for a year and the spiritual discipline you prioritized was prayer, you would hopefully see progress. If you still felt there were more ways to improve, the following year could maintain the same emphasis but with a different disciple-maker. After two years, the individual would have a wealth of material to imitate from two people on the same topic. This opportunity provides each person to make unique contributions to the life of a particular disciple.

8. **Repeatable Model** - The simplicity of the model provides the broad strokes which are easily memorized, but also provides a way for each person's plan to be different. The model allows for it

to be repeated with different emphases for an additional period of time with the same person or with a different person. As you disciple that individual, he or she is also able to take the simplicity of this approach and repeat it with another. In this way, the model is memorizable enough to help you easily multiply more disciples.

9. **Advanced Options** - Since you are merely using this framework to target your guide, you can get as sophisticated or as elementary as appropriate for the situation. In selecting a doctrine to unpack, you could wade into the simplicity of the gospel or dive deep into the more complex doctrines which we often try to avoid. Your spiritual discipline might focus on initial exposure to daily Bible reading or delve into the intensity of a longer fast. In every category, you can advance as far as you desire. This process allows you to keep the planning framework through the years as your maturity expands.

10. **Continual Investigation** - Instead of achieving a certificate of completion, this model allows for a lifelong pursuit of following Jesus. The recurrent aspect of it is so vitally important because each stage of life provides new needs for discipleship. As a person is discipled, he or she has different needs when change happens in vocational opportunities, ministry possibilities, or even family adjustments. The disobedience you fight at age 16 will probably be different than the one you need to combat at 61. The development you need to seek as a new parent will alter drastically to what you need when you are an empty-nester. Life will provide you ample opportunities to return to this drawing board and explore further growth in timely areas.

An old saying goes that you "give a man a fish, and you feed him for a day; teach a man to fish, and you feed him for a lifetime." While I believe that thinking to be a wise concept, it is unfortunately short-sighted. If you teach a man to fish, not only will he eat, but the entire village can survive, and future generations will live to see the light of day. The descendants will prove to be teachers, inventors, philosophers, pastors, doctors, workers, and all different types of people with ideas and gifts that will forever alter the course of history. Teach one man a simple yet essential process, and you will change the world.

The Distinctive Discipleship process is not intended to serve you one fish that satisfies you for a moment. This guide is not a meal but a method. Not only do I pray that maybe this framework is what you have been hoping to find, I pray that your work will impact nations yet unreached and generations yet unseen.

The destination of discipleship is the same for every individual, but each unique journey demands specific directions. If you can learn these concepts, you will have a method of making disciples that can serve you and others well regardless of your context. This model is good for an individual, better with a partner, but best with a mentor. While I know what is ideal, I would rather you do something than nothing. As you embark upon this journey, your process might involve your family, your group, or your friends. This guide shouldn't be another program but a filter through which your current activities and relationships pass through.

You know the concept, but are you ready to develop the plan? Let's begin the process of identifying where you are, and what we need to do to get you to the next spot. Say goodbye to spiritual stagnation.

CHAPTER 5 DELIGHT

"The kingdom of heaven is like a treasure hidden in a field, which a man found and covered up. Then in his joy he sells all that he has and buys that field" (Matt. 13:44).

Discipleship must be motivated by the wondrous delight of knowing Jesus. If unhealthy incentives catalyze our spiritual growth, we will eventually stall out as soon as we realize the incomplete nature of that which compelled us. Our sanctification must be prompted by delight rather than duty. Guilt tells us we have to grow; grace tells us we get to grow.

The first component is all about finding your necessary motive for discipleship. In your Distinctive Discipleship plan, you must establish the reason to grow and identify any rival to growth. Without a grasp of this category, the other five categories will serve as regimented, religious rituals. It all comes down to why do you even want to grow in the first place?

Without proper motivation, discipleship will always feel like drudgery.

We all have potential persuaders for growth. While numerous impulsions can get you going, most are severely limited to keep you going. If guilt drives you to make some changes, you will revert to old ways once your feelings of regret dissipate. If you are striving to impress someone with your spiritual prowess, the directions of your effort will rise and fall based upon the approval of others. Orthodox obligation lacks exuberant enthusiasm. Careless compliance misses willful wherewithal. Shame, fear, comparison, and expectation are all factors that can incite attempts at spiritual growth, but they each lack the fuel for longstanding endurance.

In Colossians 1:27-29, Paul spoke to the church about the ancient mystery that Christ had revealed. God's unwavering plan was to allow people very far from God to be invaded by God. Christ's authority over our lives is not because God installed him as the leader of the geographical boundaries within which we live, but because he has come as the guide to direct us as living temples on the move.

This most glorious and most precious truth of this mystery is the fact that Christ desires to dwell in us (Col. 1:27). The fullness of God dwelt in Christ (Col. 1:19), and that fullness of Christ dwells in us (Col. 1:27). The real hope of glory resides inside the life of the believer. If a person has grown accustomed to such a staggering claim, it will be challenging to drum up desire to ever progress in discipleship. If the awe and wonder of being inhabited by Christ have been lost, it will be challenging to motivate someone to prioritize intimacy with Jesus.

YOUR RATIONALE IS ESSENTIAL

A disciple must possess an endearing delight at the opportunity to follow Christ. You don't have to follow Jesus; you get to follow Jesus! The longer I follow him, the more I realize that there is no greater guide and no superior path. That is why your rationale for spiritual growth is of utmost importance.

Maintaining a disposition of delight is undeniably essential for spiritual growth. This first component seeks to eliminate any competing joys that attempt to rival our passion for Jesus. Until Jesus is installed or reinstalled on the throne of your joy, your efforts will be lackadaisical, and your affections will be inadequate.

Most Christians fail at discipleship for one of two reasons:

1. **They follow Jesus out of duty rather than delight.** If you see no desirable purpose in growth, you will suffer a miserable, religious commitment. The difference between you have to and you get to is paramount. Following Jesus is an opportunity and not an obligation.

2. **They delight in something else more than Jesus.** Some have no expendable margin to use because they have spent it on something else. Every person has a competing joy. What is it that genuinely has your affections? You love something so much that you would never miss an opportunity to enjoy it or be late to experience it. Something has your heart so much that no price is too high. Each of us has that one relationship whose approval dictates our decisions. When a greater delight is present, you cannot follow Jesus wholeheartedly.

These two can often be connected, or you might find yourself in danger of one more than the other. If you are religiously regimented, you might do the right things while lacking the necessary motivation. If you are otherly obsessed, you may resort to following Jesus at a casual pace with halfhearted efforts because you have obsessed over lesser things.

The person who finds delight in something more than Jesus doesn't comprehend who he is. Make no mistake, some of the things we love are bad things, but some of them are good things in bad positions. If your natural inclinations are towards something or someone more than Jesus, you are beginning to identify the culprit. We should not delight in anything more than Jesus because nothing can come close to the joy he brings.

What about the nature of commitment versus feelings? Many people would pushback against this concept saying that doing the right thing is better than feeling the right way. Is it possible to do the right thing but to do it in the wrong way? No one would doubt that potential. Many valid steps have been made for invalid reasons. Doing the right thing in the wrong way could actually be the wrong thing. Sinful motivations can cloud our appropriate actions.

What about the motivation of delight? What if you did the right thing but lacked the proper joy when you did it? In one sense, I have trained my mind that doing the right thing even when you don't feel like it is the highest level of commitment. In another way, I am confronted with the overwhelming reminders within the Bible regarding the importance of joy in our obedience.

Which is more critical: accepting proper duty or achieving proper delight? What if my wife told me that it meant a lot to her when I gave her flowers. As a guy, I can respond to her that it's the heart that counts and flowers don't really prove anything, but that rarely translates well. Despite my efforts, what am I to do if she says flowers mean a lot to her. What is more important – my principles or her flowers?

If I cave in and give her what she wants but fail to provide a sincere heart, she would be discouraged. She would disregard the gift due to my detached feelings associated with it. But what if I bought her flowers with joy and excitement? What if I gleefully went down the aisle trying to select her favorite colors and arrange them in a bouquet that would thrill her heart? What if I could barely contain the joy on my face as I checked out because I can envision her face the moment when she sees them? As I approach home, I can barely contain my feelings because I can't wait to see how it will make her feel. My joy is wrapped up in her joy.

I can imagine which scenario my wife would rather choose, and I believe it to be the same type of situation that God would desire as well. I have been far too guilty in my life of doing the right things absent from the right emotion. I served God more out of duty than delight. God once chastised his people not for doing the wrong thing, but for doing the right things in the wrong way. "Because you did not serve the LORD your God with joyfulness and gladness of heart, because of the abundance of all things, therefore you shall serve your enemies whom the LORD will send against you..." (Deut. 28:47-48).

Did you catch it? Their abundance in prosperity was stealing their joy in what should have been their one real delight. God's people were delighting in the gifts rather than the Giver, and while they were serving him, they lacked the beneficial joy in the process. For such neglect, God punished them. While we must often commit to proper duty even if proper delight is missing, we must prioritize the need for joy in our commitment. If the duty is mandated, the delight is unexpected. If the delight is present, the duty will follow. If God is the greatest delight of my life, I could never view any offering to him as a burden. My joy should be wrapped up in his joy.

THE RIVALED JOY

As Jesus gathered his disciples, he never asked for somber servants submitting to his rules. He invited them to become passionate participants pursuing his kingdom. Jesus taught what it would look like to possess such a proper understanding of delight. In a parable, he described a man who discovered a treasure, buried it in a field, and then sold everything he had so that he could purchase that land with the treasure safely hidden (Matt. 13:44).

> *"The kingdom of heaven is like a treasure hidden in a field, which a man found and covered up. Then in his joy he sells all that he has and buys that field"* (Matt. 13:44).

The remarkable insight about his transaction is the designation that he sold everything he had, and yet he arrived at that destitute state with joy. He was excited to get rid of all those things he held dear because there was something he valued more. He sold all that he had so that he could gain all that he wanted.

If your version of Christianity involves a miserable submission rather than a glorious opportunity, you just don't get it.

You don't have to be kind; you get to be kind. The command to stay faithful to your spouse is not to hinder your joy but to protect it. Going on a mission trip should never be a burden but a blessing. I don't have to avoid addictive behaviors, financial instability, or relational dysfunction. I get to avoid those because following Christ leads me to peace rather than chaos. How could that type of path ever lead me to drudgery?

Just like the man who sold everything he had to obtain everything he wanted, we must view Jesus as the most significant potential treasure that we could ever discover. If Jesus is the greatest delight of my life, no offering to him could ever be seen as an obligation. I will approach hard tasks with great joy if I value the benefit of accomplishment greater than the burden of the effort.

Too many people sell what they have but are miserable about it. The man in this parable was loading up his entire possessions to sell at the market with a skip in his step. The only way that you can give everything away with joy is when you value what you receive even more. The man pawned everything that he held dear without hesitation because he valued the treasure even more.

Knowing Jesus is more like finding a treasure than accomplishing a task. If your goal is to know him more, tasks feel like opportunities. That type of unbridled commitment to a more fabulous treasure is the model for what discipleship is supposed to be. Are we desirous of growth because we know it is essential for our situation or because we believe it to be advantageous to our souls? Healthy disciples can be distinguished as those who follow not because they have to obey, but because they get to obey. We must beware of items capturing our attention.

What trinket is keeping you from the treasure?

What is it in your life that you hold so tightly that keeps you from grabbing ahold of Jesus? It is that thing you think about when you first wake up in the morning and the thing that keeps you from drifting back to sleep at night. No one has to tell you to prioritize it because you naturally do so. It is your greatest ambition, your sole obsession, and the singular pursuit of your life.

Until you identify what it is and work to eliminate it or reposition it, you will struggle to prioritize discipleship at the level it deserves. Some pursuits in your life need to be removed, and you need to do so quickly. They are ungodly or unhelpful, and they are seriously hindering your walk with Jesus. Other pursuits may not require elimination but adjustment. If you have a God-given relationship in a God-sized seat, you need to reposition it rather than remove it. Ensure that your relationship with God is the filter through which every other relationship is seen and experienced.

You may already know what the rival joy is in your life. If you are still unsure, consider these questions:

1. If people observed your life over the last month, what would they discover as the most consistent devotion of your life?
2. What would cause them to arrive at that specific conclusion?
3. What does your calendar say that you prioritize?
4. What does your bank account say that you prioritize?
5. What is attempting to rival your joy for Jesus?
6. Whose approval do you seek more than anyone else?

Have you narrowed it down yet? While you may have numerous contenders, I would recommend targeting the most prevalent and dangerous rival joy present in your life currently. Whether it is a bad thing or a good thing in a bad position, you need to identify what it is and then develop a plan to address it. How would you complete this sentence?

I need to delight in Jesus more than

____________________________.

The area to address could come from anywhere. While you may share a similar rival with another person, your issue will be distinct to you at this particular time. What obsession must you address?

1. Is it an issue of **convenience**? Is it your house, your car, your wardrobe, your electronics, or your possessions?

2. Is it an issue of **commitment**? Is it your sports team, your physical appearance, your workout regiment, your successful career, or your all-encompassing hobby?

3. Is it an issue of **connection**? Is it the happiness of your spouse, the success of your children, the stability of your friendships, the approval of your mentor, or the gratitude of your church?

FINDING YOUR NECESSARY MOTIVE

Once you have established what you need to address, you must include in your plan how you are going to engage it. How will you place Jesus upon the throne of your joy? What do you need to remove, and how will you reestablish Christ where he belongs? Your plan must include objective steps rather than abstract desires. As a result of this looming issue in your life, how will you specifically partner with God?

As mentioned previously, I hesitate to give so thorough of an example that it dictates your plan. Each plan needs to be as distinctive as the individuals involved. I do think it helpful though to show a few ideas to get your mind going. Use these scenarios to help you design your plan.

- If an area of convenience has you spoiled, you probably will need to give up the rights to some of it and spend some time serving people less fortunate than you.
- If your commitment to a hobby prevents you from time with Jesus or your family, you will require some hard and fast boundaries to ensure you can determine whether you are successful or not.

- If your connection to a person hinders your relationship with God, you will have to work hard on embracing God's will over the relationship's expectation.

After you have solidified your targeted issue, create some steps in your action plan to ensure positive growth. In any scenario, you will have things you need to do, and probably some things you need to stop doing. A simple search can provide some verses to memorize or some passages with which to ground you. Ask godly leaders to point you in the direction of helpful resources like books, sermons, or podcasts that target your specific focus. If you put limits on certain activities, this step will most definitely require an aware mentor or partner seeking to keep you answerable. Even on your best days, you need someone holding you accountable to those practices deemed fit to sanctify you. As you develop some action plans, keep it a moving plan with room for alterations along the way.

You will not grow in Christ for long if he is not exalted as your supreme delight. That is why it is so critical to remove anything vying for that position. Not only is he the rightful owner of that throne, nothing else is big enough to sit in his chair.

Even if you show initial progress in discipleship, it will not last without Jesus enthroned upon his rightful centerpiece in your life. He taught us that we could not serve two masters because it will cause us to love one and hate the other (Matt. 6:24).

The most critical element in your discipleship is to make Jesus both your priority and your privilege.

You don't have to grow, but you get to grow. The reason you want to develop in Christ will determine the level of your success. Reorient your life so that you will be motivated by the wondrous delight that Christ is in you, the hope of glory.

CHAPTER 6
DISOBEDIENCE

Let not sin therefore reign in your mortal body, to make you obey its passions (Rom. 6:12).

Discipleship must warn against disobedience in any sinful leanings specific to the individual. While we all struggle with sin, we are each susceptible to deviate in different ways. For those confronting disobedience in their own lives, God provides a path of escape through every temptation. You may struggle with certain temptations for the majority of your life, but that does not mean that you have to succumb to it.

Category two in your Distinctive Discipleship plan is all about confronting disobedience. In Col. 1:28, Paul explained that a critical element in discipleship is "warning everyone." What type of warning would Paul offer to these believers? If you look at the content of his complete writings, he often divided his teaching into addressing what people were believing and how people were behaving. In many of his letters, he would start his reasoning with the doctrinal and develop his appeal into the practical. In this foundational passage that we are using for your plan, Paul highlights the need to warn everyone and then teach everyone with all wisdom. In the following chapter, we will discuss the issue of doctrine, but in this section, we must address the area of disobedience. As Paul warned those believers about sinful compromises, we need to be aware of our continual propensity to rebel against God's standards.

In our culture, we are prone to blaming everyone else for our sinful tendencies. Just like Adam and Eve pointed their fingers toward others to skirt personal responsibility, we seek to find a way out. Instead of owning our faults, we often search for any possible scapegoat to alleviate our guilt.

We will never make progress if we blame our sin on a condition or a circumstance.

While we might feel an intense leaning towards a particular sin, no one is so inclined that we are unable to pursue holiness. You can fight against temptation. Help is abundantly available. Christ didn't die for your sin so you could still cling to it. The first step in your battle is identifying which sin that you must confront.

YOUR SIN IS PROCEEDING

Disobedience is so critical to address because your sin is proceeding. The very nature of temptation is that it leads to further sinful habits. The more frequent you transgress, the less fight you put up, and the more callous you become to sin's presence (Eph. 4:19). Each person is lured away by particular passions. Desire leads to sin, and sin leads to death (Jas. 1:14).

The famous last words of many a well-intended Christian were, "it's not that big of a deal; I can stop whenever I want to stop." We seem to think we can get control of our passions, and yet we never do until some crisis warrants change. All of that which entices us keeps us on the line for more. Why is no one ever fully satisfied with their money and possessions? Does it not strike you as odd that certain items of consumption make us desperate for just one more of whatever it is? The inappropriate relationship always started as a supposedly harmless friendship. The vile content viewed began as something "not that bad."

If you think you can stop your sin whenever you want to stop it, why haven't you yet? If others confront you about it, if you know what the Bible teaches about it, and if you have seen others be devastated by a refusal to stop it, what makes you think your end will not be as disastrous? The most telling thing about your sin is the fact that you think you can handle it.

What is your most dangerous sinful leaning? All of us are prone to wander, but each of us is prone to wander in specific ways. If you are a parent of more than one child, you know this to be true. Within the early months of a child's life, you begin to determine traits and tendencies in your child that are destined to give you gray hair. What is remarkable is that siblings don't usually possess the exact set of rebellious traits. Being raised by the same parents in the same environment with the same values, and yet each of them often struggles differently. While we all sin, we all don't struggle with the same type of sin.

All of us are born into sin (Ps. 51:5), but sin manifests itself in different ways. For the person who claims to have always felt tempted in a certain way for as far as can be remembered, I believe it. Certain temptations have beguiled me, but others have never even been a serious consideration.

1. Have you experienced certain temptations for an extended period in your life?

2. Are there other issues that some people struggle with that have never even bothered you?

Your answers would probably prove my point. Some people's fuse to their temper is a short strand, while others never seem to get riled up. Certain individuals never struggle with even a hint of alcoholism, and others can't be within a mile of a bar. Some people's anxiety causes them to say, think, and do sinful things, and other people seem to have zero cares in the world.

Why is that? How can we be so different? So many factors can go into why we struggle the way we do, but the fact remains that we all sin, yet we all sin differently. In light of that reality, we all must war against disobedience, but our tactics should oppose certain temptations.

Too many people attempt to justify sin based on something they can't help or something they didn't do. Don't take the weak way out by striving to justify your sin. No one can make you do anything. We all have situations in our life that challenge our purity, but we are not rendered helpless. You might be disadvantaged, but you are not debilitated. You must decide to get real about your temptation and get specific about your fight.

It's difficult to follow Jesus when you continually allow the same sin to entangle you.

Addressing the issue of disobedience in your life is paramount for your discipleship efforts. As you attempt to continue down this path, certain sinful tendencies will seek to impede your progress. The author of Hebrews said that followers of Jesus must "lay aside every weight and the sin which so easily entangles us" (Heb. 12:1). We all get entangled with sin, but it is different sins ensnaring individual people. You wouldn't get far attempting to run a marathon with your shoestrings tied, and you won't make much progress if your spiritual steps are entangled with continual sin.

THE NAGGING TEMPTATION

In Paul's first letter to the Corinthians, he sought to help these new believers fight against some prevailing disobedience within their church. Warning against sin, he reminded the people of how Israel struggled through the temptations in the wilderness once they fled captivity. As these former slaves moved toward the freedom of the Promised Land, they experienced some pivotal moments together. Paul uses the word "all" five times to show how all of these Israelites experienced God's redemption and protection (1 Cor. 10:1-5). In a section about resisting temptation, why would Paul remind these people of God's faithfulness during the exodus? God's proven deliverance in salvation should embolden believers to persevere through temptation.

In the following paragraph, Paul reports something very different. While all experienced God's deliverance, they all did not succumb to the same disobedience. He uses the word "some" four times and implies differing ways that people sinned in the wilderness (1 Cor. 10:6-11). While the rescue was similar for all the people, the rebellion was specific to the individual.

While all of us experience the same manner of redemption, we do not all struggle with the same type of seduction.

During those trying years, different people struggled in different ways. We are no different. Redeemed by the sacrificial lamb, freed from the tyranny of an oppressive leader, blessed in every possible way, guided by good commandments, and venturing toward the security of the Promised Land, we know the incomparable glory of salvation firsthand. Yet on our journey, we must not fall prey to the former ways of life. Let us not return to slavery. Sin happens when we allow personal desires to dictate our decisions (Jas. 1:14). We all drift away from God yet in different directions. While we are all saved by the same means, we are each endangered by various vices.

Acknowledging what happened to our spiritual forefathers in the wilderness, we must learn from their mistakes and never think we are beyond similar rebellion even if it is through varying activity. "Therefore let anyone who thinks that he stands take heed lest he fall" (1 Cor. 10:12). Do you think you are invincible? Is your track record so superb that you feel yourself impervious to failure? The ones nearest to sin are often those who believe they are beyond it. There has only been one perfect person, and I am not him. Neither are you. None of us have reached an age, status, or level of maturity that insulates us from complete moral breakdown. Our only hope is if God helps us in our temptation.

> *No temptation has overtaken you that is not common to man. God is faithful, and he will not let you be tempted beyond your ability, but with the temptation he will also provide the way of escape, that you may be able to endure it* (1 Cor. 10:13).

If we can be faithful through temptation, it is because God is faithful to us. Your struggle might be unique to those around you, but it doesn't isolate you from everyone else. The baits of sin are conventional lures. We all experience the real intensity of enticements, but God promised that you would never be tempted so severely that you are unable to withstand. Whenever sin comes knocking, God always opens up another. Just like Jesus taught us to pray, we ask God not to lead us into temptation but deliver us from evil (Matt. 6:13).

God has promised to provide an escape route whenever you think sin has backed you into a corner. The devil can't make you do it. You don't have to sin. There is always a way out.

If you enter into any modern building, you will see fire escape routes posted throughout the campus. Those concerned with your safety have guaranteed, no matter where you are, there is a route out if the place sets ablaze. Similarly, every time the singes of temptation near your soul, God opens an escape hatch and points towards safety. You can endure through your leaning towards disobedience because God is faithful. If you are tired of your struggles with the same sin, I have good news for you today: God is weary of it as well and desires to help you fight against it.

We have established that we all struggle with sin in particular ways, but have you identified which one you need to address currently?

1. Do you have sins of **commission** (what you are doing) or **omission** (what you are not doing)?

2. Do you have sins of your **hands** (what you do) or sins of your **head** (what you think about)?

3. Do you have sins that are **public** (others see it) or **private** (God sees it)?

4. Do you have sins that are **continual** (I struggle all the time) or **conditional** (I struggle in certain situations)?

5. Do you feel **addicted** (I feel like I can't help myself) or **apathetic** (I just don't care to stop)?

The goal of those questions is to assist you in narrowing down the options. As you think through those scenarios, what sinful area is necessary to confront? Even if something is unknown by others, you need to work on it now if you would be mortified by others discovering it. Whatever we do in the dark, God will eventually bring to the light (Luke 8:17). Before it is exposed, why don't you repent of it instead?

Many people will claim that they have too many struggles to address. "I can't focus on just one sin because my list is too expansive." While I can believe that sentiment, I also hold that if you did some honest introspection, you know which ones are critical to addressing right now. If you don't slow down its hold in your life, the results could be catastrophic. Without going to war against it, your health, reputation, family, job, and ministry are endangered. While you might have numerous issues that need work, what is the one item that must take priority?

My disobedience that must be addressed is ______________________.

By identifying the sin that so easily entangles you, you can begin to work on a plan to get untied. While some struggles will be a lifetime battle, some of these will be seasonal. At different stages of our lives, some temptations are more pervasive than at other times. So given your context and your current struggles, how will you fight against this particular disobedience in your life?

CONFRONTING YOUR SINFUL LEANINGS

In your Distinctive Discipleship plan, you are putting together a guide that will allow you to address the most crucial areas for the sake of your sanctification. Once you make progress in one pass of your plan, you will be able to return to the same categories and address different issues. I say that to help you develop a realistic plan. If you hope to be free from all lingering sin in the next few months, you might be disappointed. If you attempt to address every single concern, you will assuredly be overwhelmed. You know what the most dangerous sinful leanings are in your life right now. I would suggest focussing on one but no more than three in your current plan. Now that you have the focus identified, it is time to establish an action plan to make progress.

1. **Get honest about your sin with God and with another person**. It is rare for someone to be embarrassed in sharing a doctrinal focus to study or a spiritual discipline to employ. Confessing your sin to another person is a challenging yet needed step.

James wrote, "Confess your sins to one another and pray for one another, that you may be healed" (Jas. 5:16). If you have secured a mentor, be honest with your shortcomings, and ask for guidance. If you have selected a partner, be authentic with your status, and ask for accountability. If you are still attempting to do discipleship on your own, I am honestly concerned about your sustained success. Please consider at least sharing your area of disobedience with one person you trust for wisdom, prayer, and accountability.

2. **Replace your sinful desire with a righteous pursuit**. The Apostle Paul's teaching consistently reminds us that in order to put something off, we need to put something on in its place. Put off the old self and put on the new self (Col. 3:9-10). As a specific example, he taught that we should put off falsehood and put on speaking the truth (Eph. 4:25). The reason this concept is so critical is that you don't want a lingering void of an activity you loved. You must replace your sarcastic comments with grateful remarks. It is necessary to stop your stealing to start your working. As you put off sinful habits, replace them with godly pursuits. Flee youthful lusts while you pursue mature aspirations alongside people heading in the same direction (2 Tim. 2:22).

3. **Fight against that sin as if your life depends on it**. We are to "abstain from the passions of the flesh, which wage war against your soul" (1 Pet. 2:11). The easiest way to lose a battle is by not acknowledging you are in a fight in the first place. You need to take your sin down before it takes you down. "For if you live according to the flesh you will die, but if by the Spirit you put to death the deeds of the body, you will live" (Rom. 8:13). Stop playing around with the stuff

> that's trying to kill you. Go to war with it. Come up with a battle strategy to confront temptation and show no mercy because sin's consequences will offer you none. As you establish a plan, make sure that your approach is as extreme as it needs to be.

In your action plan, you must articulate clear steps to fight against the most prevailing disobedience in your life. Abstract weapons never win a single battle. Get serious and get specific.

Your action plan might include different types of approaches:

- You might need to get rid of something.
- You might decide to walk away from something.
- You could use a person to walk beside.
- You need some verses to memorize.
- You must have a clear line from which not to stray.
- You might need some consequences if you disobey.

We are prone to wander, yet we are prone to wander in different ways. Your former failures don't have to be a recurring reality. For all the times you have transgressed, I want to paint a hopeful picture for you. What if instead of giving up in frustration, you went to war out of dedication? If you desire to stop living for what Christ died for, you can make progress with his help. He is eager to come to your aid. Jesus didn't die for you to continue in sin. We don't have to avoid disobedience to earn his love, but we should prioritize obedience because we already have his love.

Don't defend blatant disobedience or justify subtle compromise. Address the sin that is so easily entangling you. Sin is always regarded as a harmless habit until it becomes a devastating disaster. Realize that you must master sin, or it will master you. Get to work. Go to arms. Fight for holiness.

CHAPTER 7
DOCTRINE

But as for you, teach what accords with sound doctrine
(Titus 2:1).

Discipleship must wisely equip the follower to possess a comprehensive and competent grasp of biblical doctrine. While we all know some degree of biblical knowledge, we each should probably know a little bit more by now. Committed disciples need to strengthen any uncertain beliefs by a targeted study.

The third category of your Distinctive Discipleship plan centers on doctrine. Returning to the foundational passage for this process, Paul teaches that we are supposed to be "teaching everyone with all wisdom" (Col. 1:28). When it comes to theology, our subject matter is none other than the study of God himself. No matter how many textbooks you read, God is an inexhaustible source of truth to behold. The greatest theologian in this world still has a seismic amount of doctrinal truth to learn.

Paul's encouragement ensures that we teach not just some wisdom but all wisdom. All of us have certain books in the Bible that we know better than others. You might be more comfortable with certain concepts than others that confuse you. Our job is not to rest in what we learned in the past but to reflect upon what we need to learn in the present.

While the word "doctrine" is often used in the hallowed halls of seminary, many Christians are unsure what the term actually means. Doctrines are not lofty concepts reserved for the intellectual elite. A doctrine is simply a belief. Whether you know it or not, you have a complete set of doctrinal convictions, even if you have never acknowledged them as a doctrinal confession. You have a belief about the Bible, baptism, the Holy Spirit, marriage, and every other critical concept. Even if you are not fully confident, you do hold passionate opinions or vague notions on what you believe to be true. The pertinent issue with our beliefs is ensuring that they are actually correct.

The category focusing on doctrine is not the isolated component for the head. While you should seek to expand your mind into increasingly informed doctrinal truth, correct biblical beliefs delve into more than just cognitive comprehension. The doctrines we wrestle with in our heads become the truths nestled within our hearts. The more we understand who God is and what he can do, the closer we will desire to follow him.

YOUR CONFUSION IS DANGEROUS

How familiar are you with the Word of God? On a scale of one to ten, where would you rate yourself? Most Christians avoid classifying themselves as an intensively ignorant one or as a painfully prideful ten, so I imagine most people would place themselves somewhere in the middle.

Does that describe you? Your admission implies that you aren't where you want to be, but you are further than where you used to be. In the way that you have made progress in the past, I believe you can even make progress now. Not only is strengthening our doctrine restorative for our head to grasp the will of God, but it also mobilizes our hands to do the work of God. The world is desperate to know God, and that is why it is vital for us to comprehend the truth about him. If the Church is ignorant of the Scriptures, why are we surprised that our culture is intolerant of its claims? We can rant all day long at the way our society ridicules God's Word, but it is our responsibility to enlighten them with these biblical riches.

> **If Christians haven't adequately concerned themselves with the Bible, we should never expect the culture to affirm its truths.**

Being confused is dangerous these days. If Satan's first question to Mankind incited them to doubt God's Word, I guarantee he is tossing that question out into your subconscious as well. The entirety of history has risen and fallen on people deciding what to do with God's Word. The forbidden fruit to determine what is right and wrong is a product for sell on every cultural corner. Maintaining confusion regarding the beliefs of your faith is neither beneficial for your soul or advantageous for this culture.

When I was a college student, someone once asked if I believed everything in the Bible. As I affirmed my unwavering commitment to Scripture's reliability, I was caught off guard by the following question: "So, you believe everything in the Bible. Have you read everything in the Bible?"

If I had known that question was coming a year earlier, I might have been prepared to give a more suitable answer, but unfortunately, I was not ready. Honestly, I had been basing my entire life on a book that I had yet to finish reading. As someone raised in a local church, I had browsed bits and pieces of the Bible, but I had never adequately studied it.

- The Bible is not a yearbook. Don't go to the back of the book to look up the pages upon which you think you can find yourself.

- The Bible is not a fortune cookie. Don't assume that one sentence read at random will accurately direct your necessary next step.
- The Bible is not a biography. You are not the main character inserting yourself into every positive narrative that you conveniently claim as your own.

If you aren't confident in your ability to handle the Scriptures, that is acceptable to admit as long as you don't resort to remaining in the same state. Each of us will respond to our biblical uncertainty by either ignoring it, justifying it, or addressing it. If you ignore it, you never attempt to study the truths of God. If you justify it, you claim that you aren't smart enough, you aren't the reading type, or you lack pertinent degrees to understand such sacred matter.

If you address it, you do your best to handle the Scriptures with integrity. Paul's encouragement to his disciple Timothy is incredibly practical: "Do your best to present yourself to God as one approved, a worker who has no need to be ashamed, rightly handling the word of truth" (2 Tim. 2:15). Paul never instructed Timothy to do the best of his mentor Paul, his peer Titus, his mother Eunice, or his grandmother Lois. With the abilities and opportunities that were afforded to him, Paul expected Timothy to do his personal best. He should be able to address any question carefully because he had studied every topic diligently. His gradual preparation reduced the possibility of tragic naïveté.

You will never fortify an unstable belief by accident.

No one ever drifts toward truth; it is always a luring away. The subtle yet seismic drift happens over time. Doubting God's Word always leads to discrediting it before ultimately denying it. In your study, you are preparing yourself for whatever defense you might need to have (1 Pet. 3:15) for whenever you might need to have it (2 Tim. 4:2). More than an academic exercise, this component is essential to your discipleship. As you intentionally seek to strengthen any remaining uncertain beliefs, you engage the content of theology with your mind but embrace the author of theology with your heart.

THE UNCLEAR DOCTRINE

What is the unclear doctrine in your mind? What concept or section of Scripture do you feel ill-prepared to grasp yourself or to explain to another? The author of Hebrews gave a staggering claim regarding certain believers. In no uncertain terms, he said that many of them ought to be further along in their theological understanding than what they were at the time. They literally ought to have known better.

These believers had grown dull in their hearing of God's Word (Heb. 5:11). Whether they had become accustomed to the truth or disconnected with it, there was no vibrancy in their attempt to know God and his Word more. The Bible isn't lame. God is not boring. A dull adherence to biblical theology says more about the believer than the content. What was the author's consensus?

> *For though by this time you ought to be teachers, you need someone to teach you again the basic principles of the oracles of God. You need milk, not solid food* (Heb. 5:12).

These believers had been learning for so long that they ought to have been the teachers by that point. Instead of being able to transfer what they had learned, they required remedial reminders. Rather than providing meatier content of the word to mature believers, the author had to scale things down to a milk diet because they were still spiritual babies. Paul once told the Corinthians the same thing: "I could not address you as spiritual people but as infants in Christ" (1 Cor. 3:1). This lack of commitment to the weightier matters stunted their growth but also impacted their personal holiness. They were unskilled with the word of righteousness (Heb. 5:13). Their lack of biblical knowledge threatened their ability to display godly character.

Being unwilling to mature in doctrine not only threatens your beliefs but also your behaviors.

You will never graduate from an elementary understanding without consistent training. These believers needed to improve their discernment, but that required constant practice to acquire the ability to distinguish good from evil (Heb. 5:14). While you might think the author would then encourage them to go back to the basic principles, the opposite was encouraged. "Let us leave the elementary doctrine of Christ and go on to maturity" (Heb. 6:1). As believers, we need to mature beyond the introductory concepts. Notice we never graduate from these beginner truths, but we should advance through them.

Do you know the fundamental truths of the Bible? Are your senses trained to be able to distinguish good from evil? If you aren't developing these key areas, you are endangering yourself and others who look to you for guidance (1 Tim. 4:16).

If you look back over the previous year of your life, have you grown sufficiently in your biblical comprehension? What do you know now that you didn't know then? Most people who walk away from the faith are those who never acknowledged the complex issues and worked through them. Avoiding difficult doctrines can lead to doubtful desertions.

While the Bible is a big book, and God is a grand topic, you must decide which pivotal doctrine is essential to unpack in the coming months. You will not be proficient in all doctrinal issues, but you can be progressive in one of them. With narrowed focus and targeted study, you can make significant growth in further grasping a singular biblical doctrine. You might be wondering which doctrine to choose. Many Christians say that they believe what the Bible teaches, but they feel uncomfortable to teach those truths to someone else. Your goal must be more than mere exposure. If you hold a belief to be true but cannot express it to another, that means you don't have a complete grasp of it yet. If you cannot transfer the information to another, the doctrine may be known, but it is yet to be owned. Which doctrine will it be?

1. Is there a doctrine that is more **critical** than **curious**? As inquisitive people, we often want answers for nagging questions. While random Bible facts are interesting, they are not as crucial as other foundational issues. Don't focus on minute details if you are unable to grasp the major concepts.

2. Is there a doctrine that is more **urgent** than **useful**? You might have a situation in your life that warrants a concentrated study on a timely topic. If there is a question asked within a relationship or lingering within your culture, you might need to solidify a belief you claim to hold confidently but yet to grasp firmly.

3. Is there a doctrine I need to **review** or **rehearse**? Your doctrinal focus might be on an issue that you already believe, but you are unable to express it clearly. Your intentional study might simply prepare you to share what you know by being able to open God's Word to the exact places and concepts you need.

Is there a book you don't understand? What concept is fuzzy in your mind? Is there a section of the Bible you avoid? Do you have a doctrinal understanding that is uncertain, unclear, or unestablished? An uncertain belief can be defined, an unclear belief can be refined, and an unestablished belief can be outlined. Pick the most appropriate and necessary doctrine to unpack at this stage of your life, and get to work on it.

Focus on one belief that needs clarity. While there are plenty of options to consider, focus on one critical issue to unpack now, and the other doctrinal concepts you can address later.

The pivotal doctrine for me to study is

______________________.

STRENGTHENING YOUR UNCERTAIN BELIEFS

Your plan might focus on a beginner concept that many might know or an advanced topic that many might avoid. Major themes of theology include Bibliology (the study of the Bible), Theology (the study of God), Angelology (the study of spiritual beings), Anthropology (the study of man), Hamartiology (the study of sin), Soteriology (the study of salvation), Christology (the study of Christ), Pneumatology (the study of the Holy Spirit), Ecclesiology (the study of the Church), or Eschatology (the study of the end times). Within each of those categories, you could study numerous subtopics. Most likely, you could organize any potential biblical question within one of those general classifications above.

Once you have selected your doctrine to include in your Distinctive Discipleship plan, develop a strategy for strengthening it. Study it to the point where you could confidently share it with another. As you do your best to study, these once unclear ideas will come into focus as settled truths.

The goal is to take a vague idea and enforce it as a biblical doctrine.

If you are working with a mentor, ask for substantial resources with which to use. If you are walking beside a partner, discuss what you are learning so that you have a safe place to process it before you might have to defend it. If you are working on your plan by yourself, I would recommend summarizing what you are learning to share with others in some way. As you prepare a guide to study this doctrine intentionally, don't neglect these few helpful reminders:

1. **All books are inferior to God's Book**. Whatever your focal doctrine is, there will be numerous books on it. While there are many inspiring books, there is only one inspired book. Scripture is literally God-breathed (2 Tim. 3:16), so I would encourage you to study everything God's Word says on the matter before going to an author who tells you what he or she thinks God's Word says on the subject.

2. **Not all books are created equal**. Just because it is in the Christian living section of the bookstore does not mean it is biblical or beneficial. Some books are unhelpful, but others are downright heretical. Before you utilize additional textbooks, you should inquire about their validity from the person you trust the most who understands God's Word.

3. **Not every resource is reliable**. Just because it is in print, on a recording, or online does not mean it is legit. These days, anyone has the capacity to publish information and push it out there for others to learn from it. If you train yourself in what God's Word teaches, you will be able to discern if the resources (like the one you are holding) are accurate or not.

4. **No theologian is inerrant.** Every Christian has their favorite default theologian. Whether it is a pastor, teacher, speaker, author, or professor, don't take the shortcut and lazily align yourself with whatever your most trusted person says. Even if they

> are incredibly articulate and brilliant, they are not beyond error. None of us are. Every esteemed theologian I have ever studied has some debated or criticized belief. Don't just blindly agree with anyone. Embrace God's Word and filter what others say.

As you study and prepare, keep some journal archiving all you are learning. The goal is not to cram for a theological test in which you forget the material later. Grow in the truth so that you can go with the truth. Have the belief so cemented in your mind and ever so endearing in your heart that you are always prepared to share it with your mouth.

**If God's Word is reliable,
it can withstand any scrutiny.**

Ask the hard questions. Go into the deep places. Don't skip that chapter that challenges you. Don't avoid that book of the Bible that confuses you. Why would you want to shrink back from studying the whole counsel of God (Acts 20:27) when every single verse signifies his worth (Ps. 119:103)?

Realize that the importance of this effort is to know God and to make him known. The greatest opponents of biblical Christianity is not combatant critics but cultural conformists. The people you have to beware are those within the confines of Christianity who still echo the devil's questions from the Garden. The phrase, "Are you sure God said," has removed many from God's presence.

Wolves come in sheep's clothing (Matt. 7:15). Satan comes disguised in light (2 Cor. 11:14). Every heresy is defended by taking some Scripture out of context. All repulsive theological movements have a theme verse. While atheists ignore the Bible, heretics abuse the Bible. How do you avoid becoming one yourself? Teach what accords with sound doctrine (Titus 2:1). The more that you know the Word, the better you will know the one who wrote it.

CHAPTER 8
DEVELOPMENT

When I became a man,
I gave up childish ways. (1 Cor. 13:11).

Discipleship must address areas specific to the individual to bring about necessary development. God has created us for and called us to unique tasks. As specifically gifted and particularly positioned disciples, we each should pursue the needed maturity to do what God has called us to accomplish.

For those frustrated with a lack of maturity, you don't have to stay that way forever. In the fourth category of your Distinctive Discipleship plan, we must select a single area in your life that requires further development. Paul's unwavering commitment to the Colossian church was to "present everyone mature in Christ" (Col. 1:28). This step is all about growing up. It almost sounds as if Paul is envisioning a moment when he presents his disciples before God one day. "God, when I found these folks, they were rough around the edges, but I gave them everything I could. By my estimation, these disciples are finally mature."

Paul's goal for maturity should be ours as well. If we are reborn and start our journey as spiritual infants, we eventually have to mature. We have established that sanctification is the gradual process of holiness, so while you don't have to reach completion yet, you should be progressively flourishing. This pivotal component in your plan is not a heart issue (delight), a sin issue (disobedience), or a knowledge issue (doctrine). The necessary development component is all about improving a skill.

Most of our issues in life are due to a lack of development in some key areas. Your marriage isn't the problem, but your lack of knowing how to love your spouse adequately is widening your disconnect. Your children aren't beyond formation, but maybe your approaches are failing to connect with them. The struggles at work don't prove you are incompetent but possibly just untrained. You have something significant to offer a ministry, but you may have never honed the skills that your opportunity requires.

Some of your most significant challenges are not due to inability but immaturity.

Be encouraged. God has not called you to a task of which he refuses to provide the training and the tools. When Jesus calls us to follow him, that means we are moving somewhere. Christ is not stationary, and his followers are not intended to stagnate. In this category, we are going to find a glaring weakness in your life and systematically work towards acceptable maturity.

YOUR IMMATURITY IS LIMITING

Would you label yourself as maturing? Do you see any progress? Even if it is minimal, you want to notice how God is shaping you incrementally. You may not be where you want to be, but thank God you are not where you were.

If you ignore the weak areas in your life, they will eventually affect your strengths negatively. Any immature tendencies in your life that remain unaddressed will limit your ability to be all God has called you to be. You might be 70% mature, but the struggling 30% is making your life so incredibly challenging.

Believers too often gloss over their inconsistencies as if they are someone else's fault. "I'm just not wired like that" is an apparent jab towards God for what you to believe to be his lackluster design. "I wasn't as privileged as others" is blaming others' failures to mask personal frailties. You will never see any progress until you begin to assume some of the responsibility.

Refusing to address your areas of immaturity welcomes additional mishaps. God isn't through with you yet (Phil, 1:6), so why would you give up? The process of development is partnering together with your Heavenly Father to walk in the good works which he has prepared for you (Eph. 2:10).

As you begin to process where you need development most, your mind may gravitate towards numerous areas. While all of us have weak areas, which ones are the most critical for you to develop during this season of your life? The way that you will begin to narrow down your scope is by thinking through your specific gifts and your strategic contexts.

1. **How am I uniquely gifted?**
2. **Where am I strategically placed?**

God has given you particular gifts to use in specific places. No two people have the same design. No two people are in an identical context. When I neglect how God has prepared me and where God has positioned me, I will overlook his good and generous desires for my life.

No one else in the world is my wife's husband. No other man can be my children's dad. My church may decide to get another pastor tomorrow, but they at least have me today. In those contexts, no one else is supposed to do what God has called me to do. If I am the only one he has targeted for those tasks, have I ever considered how well I am doing?

Every believer has been prepared in specific ways and placed in specific contexts.

God has made you at this time in a certain way for a particular purpose. He isn't calling on anyone else to fulfill your unique assignment. God can work without us, but he is desirous to work with us. When God provides you with intentional abilities and specific opportunities, you can rest assured that he has exceptional plans and thrilling processes to see you through.

1. **Preparation** - Every believer has been gifted in specific ways requiring distinctive efforts for development. God has given spiritual gifts to every single believer (1 Pet. 4:10) so that we can use them for the glory of God and the good of others. Just because you have a gift doesn't mean that you know how to use it though. The person who struggles with technology can be given the most advanced gadget and yet remain unable to do the simplest of tasks. It isn't a problem with the gift but the recipient. Regarding our spiritual gifts, God has given us powerful abilities, but refusing to crack open the instruction manual can severely limit our use of them.

2. **Placement** - Every believer has been placed in specific contexts warranting unique opportunities for development. As you progress through life, you find yourself in new situations requiring new skills. If you have been hired as a defensive coordinator for a football team, you don't need to study defensive formations used on the basketball court. You work according to your responsibilities and opportunities. While you may have never considered how to serve a spouse selflessly every day of your life, you might

> want to start the training around the time you get one. When you begin your career and increase your wealth, you might need to learn how to steward what you have been given to pay the bills, save for the future, and give to Kingdom work. If you have an opportunity to serve in your church, don't just give clumsy efforts but learn how to serve to the best of your ability. Where you have been placed should dictate how you should train.

God has prepared you and placed you. The context of your life is not an accident. While you are hopefully making progress, your opportunities are too pivotal to allow mediocre advancements. Will you partner with God for your practical development?

THE PIVOTAL CONSIDERATION

To find God's direction for your life is essential. This consideration is pivotal for your discipleship. In acknowledging your opportunities, you align yourself with God to see consistent improvement.

Throughout the New Testament, the Bible teaches the importance of all believers using their specific gifts for the good of the whole. Spiritual leaders are meant "to equip the saints for the work of ministry, for building up the body of Christ" (Eph. 4:12). When everyone is using their gifts, we each contribute to one another's maturity and ministry.

> *Until we all attain to the unity of the faith and of the knowledge of the Son of God, to mature manhood, to the measure of the stature and fullness of Christ* (Eph. 4:13).

Our work is incomplete until every other disciple is fully complete. My goal is not just to experience my budding maturity but to observe yours as well. Being unified in the faith, we all grow up to a satisfactory fullness. That is why discipleship is so vastly important. Jesus did not call us to make converts but disciples. We are to continue growing and developing until the moment we finally see our Savior.

The more spiritually mature we are, the less likely we are to drift away (Eph. 4:14). Leaving childlike tendencies, we embrace biblical beliefs and behaviors. "When I was a child, I spoke like a child, I thought like a child, I reasoned like a child. When I became a man, I gave up childish ways" (1 Cor. 13:11). Maturity implies moving away from selfish, childish tendencies.

We obtain this maturity because of our intentional investment with one another. As we speak the truth in love, we experience growing maturity (Eph. 4:15). The biblical example upholds a determination to grow up in every way and not just bank on those areas that seem more manageable for us. We require loving honesty from one another to experience comprehensive development. As I develop and you develop, the entire Body of Christ further develops into God's intended design.

The more you are who God called you to be, the more others will be who God called them to be.

My wife can follow Jesus easier when I develop as a husband. My children can better understand God when I improve as a father. My church can further advance the mission when I progress as a leader. Not only is my development advantageous for my soul, but it benefits those around me. If my life impacts them and their lives impact others, who knows how far a legacy could go?

As I help another develop, I envision how God will use that person's maturity to encourage my life at a later time. When I help you improve, it ensures that someone can also further develop me. We will never regret having numerous mature disciples helping one another grow.

Let's narrow down your area of emphasis. How have you been prepared, and where you have been placed that requires further development? Don't waste your time on a skill that seems interesting to you, but you should highlight one that is important for you. If this area is a truly worthy element to emphasize, God will be glorified, and others will be thankful.

Before you select your one area to develop, consider these categories to help you focus:

1. **Family** - Regardless of what your family situation is right now, you have close relationships who deserve the best version of you. If a connection is currently strained, you could wisely focus on owning your responsibility and improving your intentionality with that person. What is the most helpful skill needed to love your family well right now?

2. **Church** - Your faith family has the responsibility to make disciples. You should be involved in that process somehow. God has given you gifts, and failure to use them robs others in your church of potential growth in their own lives. Maybe it is time to commit to a ministry and develop a helpful skill. As you serve in your church, what spiritual gift needs to be further engaged and employed?

3. **Personal** - While the previous categories are more community-based, you might also have some personal issues that you need to address. If you experience laziness or apathy toward specific skills, other areas of your life will start to feel the pain. Is there an area in your life that is complicating other areas and warrants immediate attention?

What area is most glaringly evident for you currently? Do you need to work on something that impacts your family's health, your church's growth, or your personal development? At every stage of my life, I have more immature areas than I care to admit. While you have many areas upon which you could focus, you probably have an area critical to address right now. By focusing on this crucial area, you should witness drastic improvement in your ability to display a disciple's determination for full growth.

I need development in learning how to

______________________.

Think through the condition of your life. Where is the most dangerous risk or the most significant prospect? Maybe it is time to learn how to share your faith, love your spouse, utilize your gifts, handle your finances, teach the Bible, manage your time, disciple your children, address your health, or improve your job. While these items may seem isolated to certain areas of your life, focus on the one that will impact all the others. If you abstain from developing, not only will your life suffer, but others around you will also miss out.

CULTIVATING YOUR NEEDED MATURITY

Every underdeveloped part of our life shows. All those around us feel the impact of its neglect. What part of your life needs further development right now?

If maturity is needed, don't disregard it – embrace it. Develop a plan to cultivate your needed areas of growth. As you work on this area in your Distinctive Discipleship plan, remember that this issue isn't necessarily a disobedience issue. Your skill necessary to develop might not be a sinning problem but a slacking position. The stress in your life may simply be that you haven't learned how to do something yet. As you commit to addressing this pressing issue, you will gradually see growth that should encourage you to persevere through the process.

By the nature of this plan being repetitive, the skill you develop this year probably will not repeat as the one you work on next year. As you go through different times in your life, you will experience further opportunities to advance in pivotal areas. In acknowledging your current relational responsibilities and potential opportunities, you are working on improving in key categories for the benefit of others.

The people most important to you would benefit greatly if you were more intentional with your progressive spiritual maturity.

No one will complain about you becoming more like Jesus. They might actually join you in the process. Your example will benefit their lives and probably stimulate their growth.

With the skill in mind, how do you plan to mature in this area?

1. **Establish the Motive** - You need to articulate why this skill is essential. Without a God-honoring motive, you might lose interest along the way.

2. **Search the Scriptures** - If this skill is worth developing, I guarantee the Bible at least provides principles with which to direct you. Discover what God says regarding your area of development.

3. **Define the Goal** - Abstract hopes rarely produce concrete goals. Be able to share succinctly what you are hoping to accomplish and how you will be able to determine success.

4. **Interview the Experts** - Find the people who do that skill the best and learn from them. You don't need to reinvent the wheel when surrounded by people who are already rolling.

5. **Collect the Resources** - Working with experts and other trusted mentors, collect a reasonable amount of resources to study during this process. Get the best material in your hands and get to work.

6. **Implement the Steps** - In addition to the goal, you need to have some mile-markers guiding your efforts along the way. Without some clear waypoints, you may get discouraged about the length of the task.

7. **Recognize the Progress** - If you see actual change, don't hesitate to celebrate it. Once you notice progress, you will be motivated to continue the process.

At the end of this cycle with your Distinctive Discipleship plan, you may not exhibit mastery over an area, but you should show maturity. If someone looked over those focused months, they should see tangible progress in your ability to work at your gifting within your environment. Work on aligning your development with his calling.

God did not randomly gift you or haphazardly position you.

If God has a purpose for how he made you and where he placed you, take confidence in the fact that he will complete what he started. He is committed to seeing us through. We are merely joining him in that effort.

From taking our first steps to learning advanced skills, the first attempts were always pitiful. Despite the rough beginnings, the more we practiced something, the more natural it became. We made clumsy efforts with calculated attempts until they became confident skills. In the area you seek to develop, don't get discouraged if it isn't natural at first. Good things rarely are. As you continue to put forth the effort and see progress, you can glory in the God who doesn't give up in light of our mishaps.

CHAPTER 9

DISCIPLINE

...discipline yourself for the purpose of godliness (1 Tim. 4:7).

Most people don't grow in their faith simply because they don't want it bad enough. Sure, you might feel guilty that you should be further along than you are right now, but that awareness does not necessarily guarantee transformation. You really have to get frustrated before you truly get going. Many Christians wrestle with remorse, but few engage in alteration. You will never really experience success in your spiritual formation without rolling up your sleeves and getting to work.

The fifth category of your Distinctive Discipleship plan is focusing on discipline. As Paul described his discipleship efforts, he commented, "for this I toil" (Col. 1:29). If that sounds laborious, it is because spiritual improvement does require work. The blood, sweat, and tears of discipleship often come through this critical commitment to discipline.

It's not the type of discipline that serves as a punishment for wrongdoing. This type of discipline is the process of going to the spiritual gym and sweating through the exercises that develop your faith formation. Through regular training, intended to create a sense of ritual, and challenging increases, ensuring the presence of tension, you begin to see gradual progress. What makes most of these exercises difficult is because you most often do them where no one else notices. People may see the effects of your spiritual disciplines, but, if done correctly, they will rarely see the effort.

Christians have set exercises that are essential for sanctification. While the list may vary from person to person, standard practices such as Bible study, prayer, Scripture memorization, fasting, giving, and others appear often. While delight focuses on a desire, disobedience focuses on a temptation, doctrine focuses on a belief, and development focuses on a skill, discipline focuses on a practice.

With thoughtful intentionality, these practices form individuals into stronger disciples. The diligent reps in spiritual workouts reveal their effectiveness when life's competitions begin. As the work in the gym shows its effectiveness on the field, the commitment to the disciplines reveals their value behind closed doors.

YOUR GROWTH IS HINDERED

Every dedicated disciple must employ spiritual disciplines in order to grow for the long haul. Through these disciplines, you train the habits necessary for your soul. Considering the category of spiritual disciplines, are you presently satisfied with your current commitment?

I remember the moment on my journey that I got sick and tired of being sick and tired. Serving on my first international mission trip, I was languishing something I learned during training. Surrounded by incredible mentors, I finally realized that I wasn't as grounded as I thought I was. My story did include training, but something was obviously missing. I thought I knew the Bible until I was around some people who really understood it. I had never felt embarrassed to pray in public, yet when I heard these mentors pray, they spoke as if God was in the room right beside them. They required no search engine to remember biblical truth because they had committed so much to memory.

I remember one Bible study to which a mentor invited me. As we approached the gathering, I noticed he had forgotten his personal Bible. So that he wouldn't be embarrassed, I asked if he needed to borrow mine. He declined my offer because the study consisted of him fielding our questions about the Bible and him forming every answer from verses he had memorized. Through every random question, he veered through every corner of the Bible by memory, and I didn't know if I should be motivated or devastated. As I saw the gap between us, I embarked upon the mission trip with guilt because I should have been further along than I was at that point.

As I wallowed in my spiritual despair, two men of a different faith approached our team one day. We were sent to evangelize people, but these well-prepared missionaries came seeking to evangelize us. These men really knew what they believed. Preparing for a followup encounter, my teammates and I remarked, "I sure wish our mentors were here for this conversation. They could handle these guys with no problem."

One guy in our group commented, "What do they have that we don't? We have access to the same Bible. We possess the same Holy Spirit."

While my friend's comments were reassuring to engage in the looming next assignment, we were also painfully aware of our unpreparedness. While believers may all be granted access to the Bible, we are all not as familiar with it. As I struggled through that encounter, I so desperately wished I had taken spiritual disciplines more seriously so I would have been ready for such an opportunity.

An old saying goes that 'The best time to plant a tree was twenty years ago. The second best time is now." If you are like me, I am sure you wish you could rewind the years and commit to some practices that would have better prepared your current confidence. Unfortunately, we cannot travel back in time and make those changes. While I wish I had started studying the Bible seriously twenty years before that encounter, the only thing I could do on that day was rethink my present priorities.

Instead of regretting where you are, let's make some plans to ensure you don't stay there. If you know that you should be further along in spiritual disciplines by now, don't let personal condemnation rob you of immediate mobilization. Instead of lamenting what you neglected in the past, why not focus on what you can develop in the present? If you spent the next year of your life focusing on training your soul with one spiritual discipline, your next twenty years would be drastically different.

Spiritual disciplines are premeditated activities that encourage spiritual growth.

The type of formative spiritual actions that shape you do not take place by accident. You don't stumble into the gym, and you will not wander into these activities by chance, either. Disciplines are those exercises that you plan for, commit to, and engage in for a tangible result. We usually associate premeditation with crimes that were thought through before they were ever committed. Premeditated spiritual efforts are those contemplative commitments decided in your mind before practiced with your hands.

Discipleship must train in areas of spiritual discipline for continual growth. You will experience spiritual milestones that provide a turbo boost of growth, but those moments are rare and unpredictable. Spiritual experiences can catalyze your faith, but spiritual disciplines furnish the lifeblood for your longevity. Every dedicated disciple must employ spiritual disciplines in order to grow for the long haul. Through these disciplines, you train the habits necessary for your soul. The more intense your training, the more successful you will become.

Are you currently satisfied with your commitment to spiritual disciplines? Very few people would say they have arrived in that department. More people feel a sense of shame rather than a sense of accomplishment when speaking of such matters.

We might say that we believe in the importance of spiritual disciplines, but without the commitment to verify those claims, we are merely offering lip service. If we cannot find time for spiritual training, we are investing our lives into something we value more. You do have the time to grow; you are just spending those moments on some activity that you hold more dear.

How many hours have you lost to meaningless activity? You can enjoy material things in this life, but not so much that you neglect spiritual matters. It is unnecessary to quit your job to become active in spiritual disciplines. A mere fifteen minutes a day focused upon one effort would alter your life dramatically.

Many lose interest in spiritual habits because they promise gradual progress in a world which sells immediate results. We want quick fixes, but these habits are designed to make a difference for the long haul. Just like any weight loss program that promises instantaneous results with minimal effort has little chance at providing you with any enduring change, any promise of spiritual steroids are destined to fail. You might see a quick bump, but you will not experience spiritual health.

THE CRITICAL DISCIPLINE

At different times along my journey, I experience additional motivation for growth. During those times, I find myself eager to master every possible discipline. Some of my most treasured

Christian books assist believers in how to improve in every single practice. The only problem with such a format is that I can't make progress in one area because I am overrun with needs in all areas. After one chapter makes me feel guilty about my lack of prayer, I begin intercessory boot camp only to read the next section on Scripture memory and start to overextend myself.

Instead of attempting to flex your spiritual muscles in all disciplines, I want you to focus on one for your Distinctive Discipleship plan. Whether it is a first step towards reading the Bible regularly or an advanced effort to memorize a book of the Bible, I want you to select the critical discipline that you must train during this time in your life. You hopefully will be able to strengthen all of these over time, and you will have as long as God sustains your life to do so. Yet given your current spiritual health and circumstantial condition, you must determine what discipline is the most essential to develop.

Why should you prioritize spiritual disciplines? The answer to that question will determine your level of success. If you are seeking someone's approval, your motive will counteract against your efforts. If guilt is your driving factor, you will quickly see that it can only get you so far. If you feel as if your commitment to disciplines provides something for God instead of offering something to you, your growth will be severely limited. If your goal is anything other than godliness, then your spiritual disciplines will be more drudgery than delight.

Spiritual disciplines are not meant to make you more liked by Jesus but to make you more like Jesus.

Don't miss this vital truth. God's love for you is not contingent upon your performance for him. He has not reserved his affection for the disciplined few. When you engage in disciplines, you are not attempting to earn something from God. He has already given you everything you need. The actual ability to engage with God through spiritual disciplines is the glorious reward.

As Paul encouraged his disciple Timothy, he reminded him that the purpose of spiritual disciplines is nothing more than godliness (1 Tim. 4:6-7). Any other motive will lead to frustration. If you are frustrated with your ungodly tendencies, then engage in godly practices.

> *For while bodily training is of some value, godliness is of value in every way, as it holds promise for the present life and also for the life to come* (1 Tim. 4:8).

I believe that everyone thinks their bodies could be in better shape than current reality. Despite the possible work needed, our souls need more work than our bodies. Bodily training advances you in this life; godly training advances you in this life and in the one to come! For those so committed to their physical appearance, imagine the health of their souls if they spent as much time developing it as they focused on their body.

Even though Timothy was a young pastor, Paul never gave him a free pass to neglect hard work. Never use your age or experience to serve as an excuse (1 Tim. 4:12). Some of us didn't have the example before us, so let's leave one for the people behind us. Paul encouraged Timothy to focus on these disciplines so that he would experience gradual yet significant transformation. "Practice these things, immerse yourself in them, so that all may see your progress" (1 Tim. 4:15). Practice doesn't make perfect; practice makes progress. You cannot lead a biblical life if you do not know biblical truth, and the more that you work out your faith with spiritual disciplines, the greater results you will regularly experience.

While you will notice changes, your example will also inspire others to make changes of their own. Your spiritual habits will impact you and influence those around you (1 Tim. 4:16).

Someone is learning from your practices. Would you want those closest to you to copy your example and paste it into their lives? If you would not be happy with their spiritual potential with such a scenario, then it is time for you to make a change.

- Those closest to me will either notice dust or fingerprints on my Bible.
- Others will notice how natural or awkward my prayers sound.
- I will respond to others' questions with either my opinion or God's Word.

What will be the next spiritual discipline you begin to improve? While different ministries, churches, or denominations have certain ones they emphasize, major habits seem to frequent most lists. Some of the most common spiritual disciples are Bible reading, prayer, Scripture memory, fasting, worship, giving, Sabbath rest, service, evangelism, and church involvement. Maybe you could think of an additional one or two. Within each of these habits, there are initial steps as well as advanced practices. What will your next discipline be?

I will focus on the spiritual discipline of

______________________.

Focus on one spiritual discipline that will revolutionize your life. Show restraint from attempting too much at once, but don't settle for a meager goal either. Get to work and notice the change.

TRAINING YOUR SOUL'S HABITS

Instead of being overwhelmed by working on all disciplines, prioritize strengthening one for the next few months. As you make progress in one area, it will hopefully become a natural part of your life. After the practice becomes second nature, you can work on an additional discipline in your next plan or further the one you are working on now.

Prioritizing one discipline as a dedicated activity will eventually transform it into a joyful habit.

Make this discipline something you decide to do until it becomes something you want to do. You will not always wake up in the morning eager to discipline yourself, but do it anyway. I have made excuses as to why I shouldn't engage in the disciplines, but I have never once regretted it once I completed it. Don't assume you will make progress if you don't have a strategy. As you select your discipline, make sure you have thought through action steps to include with your plan.

1. **Plan** - Your schedule can get hectic, and your interests can become divided. By making a plan of how you will work on this discipline, you can set yourself up for success. Make it a priority to redeem your time (Eph. 5:16).

2. **Partner** - Find someone to keep you accountable for your efforts. Let this person sharpen (Prov. 27:17) and encourage you (Heb. 10:24). Whether it is your spiritual mentor or your accountability partner, make sure you have given this person specific goals with which to gauge your progress.

3. **Persist** - Don't quit if you missed a goal or neglected a practice. If you missed yesterday, don't let that hinder you from today. Righteous people are those who fall and get back up again (Prov. 24:16). Just pick back up where you left off and get back to work. Godliness is the goal – not a continuation of a streak.

4. **Present** - Don't keep all you are learning to yourself. Present something that you are learning from this discipline to someone else. Whether you share it through a conversation, letter, message, social media, or another outlet, learn to communicate your lessons to others (Ezra 7:10; 1 Cor. 11:1).

Eventually, your discipline will become a delight. You won't have to do the discipline; you will get to do the discipline. Until that time comes, don't give up!

Immerse yourself in training with one spiritual discipline that is essential for your soul's health.

When I think back to my panicked state on that first mission trip, I remember how my mentor's example inspired me to put down my excuses. I wasn't ready for that encounter, but I vowed I would prepare myself for the next one. I found a collection of note cards on a key chain and began to memorize Scripture. With the words on one side and the reference on the other, I was amazed at how quickly I could make progress with something once I was motivated.

Years later, I had missionaries from that same faith approach me unannounced at my house on a Saturday morning. I wasn't expecting them, but I finally was prepared for them. As they asked me questions, verses tucked away in my mind from years earlier were prompted by the Holy Spirit (John 14:26). The discipline of Scripture memory was equipping me to do what I wished I could have done years before.

As they left that day, I realized how long it had been – twenty years. On the other side of the world, I wished I had planted that tree years before, but instead, I put a seed in the ground on that day. It produced what I needed right when I needed it. It can for you too. Train your soul's habits now and reap the benefits later.

CHAPTER 10
DEPENDENCE

"I am the vine; and you are the branches. Whoever abides in me and I in him, he it is that bears much fruit, for apart from me you can do nothing" (John 15:5).

Your plan is taking shape. Through this narrowing down process, you almost possess a complete Distinctive Discipleship plan with which to initiate. Up to this point, you have focused on five categories: a delight to pursue, a disobedience to control, a doctrine to clarify, a development to enrich, and a discipline to exercise. While these five priorities are essential to a comprehensive growth strategy, you will not experience any longterm success without the final component.

In your Distinctive Discipleship plan, the sixth category is all about dependence. In our focal passage, Paul describes his personal toil as "struggling with all his energy that he powerfully works within me" (Col. 1:28). So while he was working intensely, he never thought for a moment that his efforts were detached.

If any level of spiritual success was possible, it was because God was empowering him for his personal growth and his intentional efforts in discipling others. He was working with all of his might while understanding that every bit of his power came from God. The strength he applied was the power that God had supplied.

Discipleship must continually acknowledge the complete dependence upon Jesus for the believer's maturity.

As Christians, we will never obtain such a status where we can manage by our own power. Even among increasingly maturation efforts, we never reach the point where we can depend upon our strength. Apart from Jesus, we can do nothing. No matter our age, level of experience, or evidence of progress, we are still desperate for God to help us with the simplest of tasks.

YOUR AWARENESS IS LACKING

Before you begin to determine which focus goes in this category, you must settle one critical issue in your mind: who is ultimately accountable for your spiritual growth? Is God responsible, or are you responsible? The answer is yes.

While that answer may seem frustrating at first, it is necessarily critical to embrace as reality. The essential element of this process is the acknowledgment of a partnership. Sanctification is the divine's part of growth, while discipleship is the disciple's part of growth. God is working in our lives to make us more like Jesus, but he uses our efforts significantly towards that end.

How accountable are you for your spiritual growth? On each side of this question exists two dangerous extremes. You can either deny all responsibility or accept all responsibility.

1. **Entitled people reject the responsibility for their personal spiritual growth**. In a time when so much is handed out to so many, plenty of disciples struggle with accepting personal responsibility. So many people are raised in an environment where

parents cater to every desire, leagues provide trophies for every participating team, teachers are pressured to pass failing grades, bad behavior is excused due to complicated conditions, and employers must include numerous perks into a package. In such a setting, why are we surprised that our churches are full of people thinking that spiritual growth happens by mere exposure to quality content and seasoned professionals? Entitlement leads to idleness.

2. **Independent people assume the responsibility for their personal spiritual growth**. To the other extreme, we must beware of acting as if everything of value is somehow dependent upon us. The disciple desirous of growth must avoid immobility as well as independence. Completion of a class does not guarantee the acquirement of a skill. Just because you memorized a verse does not mean that you have applied it. If you are attempting to live for Jesus without Jesus, you are ultimately missing the point. You must take the initiative to grow without taking the credit for it.

Somehow we must find balance. Can we discover a way to utilize effort while relying on his strength? Is it possible to improve our attempts while desperate for his presence? Apparently, it is because Scripture repeatedly calls for it.

Effective disciples are those who work hard with God's power working hard through them.

My most significant times of growth are never when I am feverishly working through spiritual to-do lists isolated from the Spirit or when I am lackadaisically debilitated to do anything because I expect God to do all the work. The most spiritually enriching times of my life have been when God was at work within my work. I saw considerable growth when my efforts were directed and driven by the presence and power of God. Scripture is full of similar evidence.

- When God asked Moses to speak, the shepherd was staggeringly hesitant due to his inadequacies. God didn't provide Moses with false assurance to trust in personal abilities, but he offered reliable encouragement in the trustworthiness of God's unwavering capabilities (Ex. 4:12).
- When God sent Joshua to take Jericho, his strategy didn't focus on the spears and the swords. Instead, he employed the priests and the trumpets. With such an unexpected approach, the Israelites never earned the victory but instead received it (Jos. 6:2).
- When Gideon gathered forces to combat the Midianites, the LORD intentionally decreased the size of his army. He reduced the troops because he didn't want Israel thinking their military might had delivered themselves (Jud. 7:2).
- When Paul continued his missionary journeys, he experienced torment and asked God to alleviate it. Unwilling to remove the hindrance, God expected Paul to continue the work and witness what God could do with a weakened minister (2 Cor. 12:7-10).

While God would do the work, Moses still opened his mouth, Gideon still charged the battle line, Joshua still circled Jericho, and Paul still journeyed to the nations. When miraculous things happened in all of those scenarios, there could be no question as to who should receive the credit. While the power was obviously from God, he shared the experience with his servants. God prizes doing extraordinary things through ordinary hands.

As we work out our salvation, we realize that it is God who works in us (Phil. 2:12-13). He works within our work! If any good comes from our lives, we readily acknowledge that we have no good besides God (Ps. 16:2). "For who sees anything different in you? What do you have that you did not receive? If then you received it, why do you boast as if you did not receive it?" (1 Cor. 4:7). No matter how valiant or pitiful our efforts are, we realize our position and know where to establish the acclaim. If it was a pathetic result, we should take the blame. If it was a mesmerizing success, we are unable to take the credit.

THE INCAPABLE CONFESSION

How noticeable is your growth right now? If you can hit the right stride of aligning your efforts with God's power, you are probably witnessing an undeniable transformation. If you focus on one extreme to the neglect of the other, you are undoubtedly experiencing consequential disappointment.

As Jesus gathered his disciples for his final lessons before his death, he knew the urgency of the hour even if they were yet oblivious. For all his explanations and warnings, they were still distressed and disoriented at the events surrounding his crucifixion. During the Last Supper, he explained how desperately they needed to make a critical realization. They were utterly incapable of living for God without the presence of God, and so are we.

Jesus claimed to be the vine, and his disciples serve as the branches (John 15:5). These first-century Jewish men didn't miss the connotation Jesus made. The prophet Isaiah once described Israel as a great vineyard that was intended to bless others. Connection to God's people would undoubtedly incur a spiritual ripeness. Unfortunately, it failed by yielding wild grapes instead of the luscious produce it was supposed to provide (Isa. 5:2).

For so much of Israel's history, the people focused on connecting to the religion rather than the Redeemer. When Jesus claimed to be the "true" vine (John 15:1), he was emphatically expressing that regimented religious rituals would not suffice. If you want to know God, you have to go through Jesus. He isn't an association of the faith but the point of it all. Jesus promised that God would remove every fruitless branch and prune every fruitful branch (John 15:2). It is remarkable to hear how God will work with every person based upon the type of fruit we produce. Connection to a religion about God without a relationship with God will never sustain life.

> *"I am the vine; you are the branches. Whoever abides in me and I in him, he it is that bears much fruit, for apart from me you can do nothing"* (John 15:5).

Jesus knew of our deep need. We are lost without him. I am incapable of doing anything spiritually worthwhile in my own strength. You are unable to do anything on your own either. We are called to abide, remain, or dwell with the person of Christ, or we are sunk. Abiding in Christ is the believer's commitment to utter dependence upon Jesus.

Our dependence on Christ does not imply inactivity but promotes diligence to those things which strengthen our connection. As we abide in Christ and his words abide in us, our prayers are in line with his desires (John 15:7). Our level of desperation upon the Word of God and the presence of God reveals our comprehension of how great he is and how insignificant we are. We would each fare better with less activity and a stronger connection than more busyness and a weakened connection.

> **Your spiritual growth is contingent upon how intently you protect your connection to Jesus.**

The more connected we are to Jesus, the more fruitful we are (John 15:8). The more productive we are, the greater our joy proves to be (John 15:11). The efforts made for our spiritual growth might be difficult, but they should not be dreadful. When we realize that these efforts connect us closer to the source of life, it should produce sheer joy for every inch that we draw near.

These pivotal lessons from Jesus are uniquely timed. As he walked beside them for three years, you would assume he would have given these instructions to them in the initial months. With only moments away from his arrest and hours before his death, he urges them to say near. How could they do that? He was about to die. Staying close to him would no longer be an option. Even once he resurrected, he would thereafter ascend into heaven. Why wait till a time to emphasize abiding with him when they wouldn't be able to experience that reality any longer?

The principle of the message and the nature of its timing should serve as enthralling news for us. If Christ's departing words included a command for those disciples to stay close to him, that means we can as well. Jesus was highlighting something even closer than physical proximity. He was emphasizing spiritual intimacy.

Jesus encouraged us to abide with him and have his words abide in us (John 15:7). As we commit to that closeness, he promises that he will answer our prayers. Directed and fueled by the Word of God, our prayers will possess a marked clarity and an uncharacteristic boldness. A disciple who is filled with the Word of God knows exactly what to pray and how to pray. When we know the desires of God, we don't pray about them timidly.

In this sixth and final category of your Distinctive Discipleship plan, you are to select a focus with which to practice abiding with Christ. As you do your part of this work, what are you praying for God to do? His undeniable power and unthinkable wisdom should cause us to commit all things to him through prayer, but there may exist specific issues of which prayer is the only option. With some circumstances, it's not that you won't do anything, but you honestly can't do anything.

As you undertake your specific plan to secure spiritual growth, what are you praying for God to do that only he can do? This category focuses on a prayer need. While the discipline category might seek to develop the practice of your prayer life, this dependence category focuses on one prayer request associated with your growth.

You might ask God to do something beyond your control or outside your influence.

1. **Beyond Your Control** - Is there something you want God to do that you honestly can't affect? It might be an issue of your heart, mind, soul, or strength that you need him to address. If there is a legitimate need you have that is beyond your control, have you prayed about it?

2. **Outside Your Influence** - Is there a prayer need you have that is outside of your influence? It might be related to a strained relationship, a challenging circumstance, or a potential opportunity. As this issue is nothing you can fix personally, have you prayed about what God would do?

As you think through those two categories, hopefully, you can narrow down numerous prayer concerns to some pivotal requests which you need to lay before God.

My prayers of dependence will ask God to

______________________.

Are you dependent upon God? Have you acknowledged your desperate need? Through this prayer focus, you will archive your requests and God's activity. You are praying for something to change that will positively impact your spiritual growth. His involvement in your life will hopefully cause you to pray even more. As you see him move in powerful ways, you will be reminded of how you can trust him for anything at any time.

ACKNOWLEDGING YOUR DESPERATE NEED

It wasn't long after moving into an older home that we realized more renovations were needed than originally expected. Working through a growing punch list, we had our work set out for us. One day, I was stunned as I noticed water coming through our playroom ceiling. With every passing moment, the drips turned more into a downpour. As I feverishly bounded up to the attic, I realized that the water heater had burst, and fifty gallons of water needed somewhere to go.

After slowing the currents, I began to investigate how this happened. During the process of buying the home, the inspector looked for the release piping that drains the water in such an incident. Nestled there in the attic, the pipes were laid right beside the water heater. They just were never connected. Placed a few inches away was the connection that would have saved us from a costly calamity.

Many discipleship stories sound awfully similar. When trouble hits, everyone looks around to how it could have happened. The damage is so widespread, and people wonder how it ever got to such a critical place. All the person needed was a simple connection to an available help. The potential to avoid ruin was present the entire time.

I pray that your Distinctive Discipleship plan has some aggressive yet reasonable goals. No one wants to stay the same, and I am sure you have listed some areas for growth that could be real game-changers for you. If you implement all that you hope you can, you should experience steady yet significant advance.

In all your impressive efforts, if you fail to stay connected to Jesus, you will be unable to experience legitimate transformation. You might be busy, but you probably won't be successful. You must learn to abide with him.

Doing works for Jesus is different than doing works with Jesus. At times in my life, I have been so busy for Christ that I have missed him in the process. If discipleship is about following Jesus, you cannot do it by charting your own path and journeying at your own pace. If you really want to grow closer to him, he should obviously be involved in the process.

Your proximity to the King is directly proportional to your productivity for the Kingdom.

If you want to witness a God-sized work in your life that changes you and others, you have to remain connected to the source. The people who experience the most significant growth are those with the smallest distance from God. So as you toil with all of his energy which he will provide you, how are you praying for him to move? What dependent prayers are you praying? Show some sincerity and desperation in your prayers. God can tell if you are praying because you are supposed to pray. In contrast, he knows when you are praying out of sheer desire to connect with him and to watch him do only what he can do.

As you commit your entire plan to God in prayer, it also includes a specific item or two that you are entirely reliant upon him to accomplish. This request is something you admit that you cannot do in your power. In your prayers, make sure that your requests are specific (avoid making generic requests) and surveyable (pray with targeted expectation). As you work for Jesus while walking with Jesus, you will begin to notice his intentional involvement in your life. Once you get used to this proximity, you should never fathom attempting discipleship ever again removed from the original disciple-maker.

CHAPTER 11
IDENTIFIABLE PROGRESSION

And I am sure of this, that he who began a good work in you will bring it to completion at the day of Jesus Christ (Phil. 1:6).

If we are to obey the message of Jesus, complete discipleship of the whole person is our mandate. Our goal is to present every single believer mature in Christ (Col. 1:28). Many Christians have often talked about discipleship more than we have practiced it. In our search for a perfect approach, we have often neglected tangible opportunities right in front of us.

Over the last few chapters, I have given you a guide. It's not a perfect plan, but at least it is a practical one. Using Colossians 1:27-29, you have six categories to filter your current needs to design a Distinctive Discipleship plan for the next few months of your life.

While the previous chapters have fleshed out the concepts to produce greater comprehension and retention, the process is straightforward. If you can remember those verses and categories, you can help any person anywhere in the world create a guide with which to disciple him or her. After one pass of the plan, you can step back and evaluate the progress and start over again. Depending upon the previous success, you may work on six new targets or continue some of the prior ones if not sufficiently addressed. The plan is an adaptable, memorizable, and repeatable process with which you can experience personal growth or encourage growth in another.

Taking into consideration that unknown opportunities and challenges loom ahead in our lives, we will be able to use this guide no matter what comes our way. During every stage of experience, we can ride every success and confront every failure with this balanced approach for comprehensive growth. Since generalized attempts cannot address unique individuals, developing a distinctive guide will help guarantee that you prioritize and plan for discipleship.

Your spiritual health at the end of your life will be determined by how diligent you are right now.

If you want to grow, you can grow. You don't have to stay stuck any longer. By identifying any needed areas and establishing a specific plan, you can make continual and substantial progress in the things that matter most. As you experience gradual transformation, you cannot take the full credit or give the complete blame for your spiritual condition. God is doing the heavy lifting for your sanctification, but you are reasonably responsible as well for your discipleship. While you will have things challenging your growth, you cannot farm out your responsibility. The more diligent your efforts are, the more prominent your progress will be.

EVERYTHING YOU NEED

While there may be some additional things you want in your spiritual life, I believe that you have absolutely everything you need to start growing. If God is for you, what could stand against you (Rom. 8:31)? God wants you to grow even more than you want to grow, and he will not withhold anything necessary from you to be successful.

When I first joined a gym, I noticed the vast array of individuals present. Some participants were infrequent attendees who did minimal strenuous activity. Other members were consistent in their attendance and ever-increasing in their displays of strength. While some merely wanted to coordinate intentional movement, others wanted to achieve drastic improvement.

As I noticed these fitness fanatics, someone would often remark incorrectly regarding the impressive quality of their muscles. “Look how many muscles that guy has!” In reality, God gives every person approximately 650 muscles. No one person has more muscles than another. Some people do more with the muscles they have been given. The state of a person’s physical condition is dependent upon how diligent an individual applies effort. Muscles are given by God, and then they are strengthened by you. If you are a child of God, every necessary spiritual muscle is at your disposal. The question is – will you engage in spiritual training and work those muscles out?

I often create an unhealthy divide between myself and the heroes of the faith. When I study the accounts of these biblical legends, their testimonies seem so matchless to me even despite their rampant failures. While Abraham, Moses, David, and Peter all had unfortunate moments in their stories, I, unfortunately, place these faith icons in an untouchable category.

Take Peter, for example. Even if it was for a brief moment, the man walked on water. Jesus allowed him to behold his luminous transfiguration. Peter’s initial sermon on Pentecost saw higher response numbers than were ever recorded during the ministry of Jesus. This man was a remarkable disciple.

Yet, in his later days, he removed the inapproachable barriers for all present and future believers. He wrote, “to those who have obtained a faith of equal standing with ours by the righteousness of our God and Savior Jesus Christ” (2 Pet. 1:1). All believers have an equal standing with the likes of the water-walking, transfiguration-beholding, Pentecost-preaching Apostle Peter? How can that possibly be? Peter knew this to be true because our status comes not by an individual's record but by the Savior's righteousness. The grace of Jesus puts all believers on a level playing field.

No Christian has a different standing before God than another. Take all the disadvantages with which you started, and you are still primed to experience unfathomable progression within your lifetime. If you doubt your ability to grow, that is more of a criticism of God's power than an indication of your resolve. No biblical hero or historical legend has superior opportunities that surpass your own.

Jesus even told his disciples and those that would follow, "Truly, truly, I say to you, whoever believes in me will also do the works that I do; and greater works than these will he do, because I go to the Father" (John 14:12). Should we truly anticipate experiencing greater things than what Jesus experienced? Peter saw that in his lifetime, and we should expect nothing less than that as well.

> *His divine power has granted to us all things that pertain to life and godliness, through the knowledge of him who called us to his own glory and excellence* (2 Pet. 1:3).

God has given you everything that you need to grow. No Christian lacks anything necessary to live a godly life. If you need help to navigate life and require assistance to strengthen godliness, I have good news for you – God's divine power provides it all.

When the gospel changed you, you received something more than a ticket to heaven. Salvation is more than avoiding hell once you die, but it is embracing heaven as you live. God's promise stands true that he has put every necessary tool in your hands to improve in all areas that pertain to life and godliness. He is calling us to follow him by his own glory and excellence, and he will not leave us stranded on that path.

The gospel saves us in an instant, but discipleship sanctifies us for a lifetime. Since we are incomplete, we should still be working towards the acquisition of all that our calling upholds. Peter taught to "make every effort to supplement your faith" with a list of favorable characteristics (2 Pet. 1:5-7):

- **Virtue** - cultivating **development**
- **Knowledge** - clarifying **doctrine**
- **Self-Control** - confronting **disobedience**
- **Steadfastness** - engaging **discipline**
- **Godliness** - establishing **dependence**
- **Love** - securing **delight**

Our faith is sufficient for salvation, but discipleship is necessary for sanctification. As Peter taught, we should seek to supplement our faith with traits beneficial to our growth. Pursuing progress in these key areas proves God's tangible work in our lives. Peter wrote that "if these qualities are yours and are increasing, they keep you from being ineffective or unfruitful in the knowledge of our Lord Jesus Christ" (2 Pet. 1:8). Every person's discipleship could be categorized as either increasing or ineffective.

You are not there yet, but are you getting there? Is your faith increasing? Is your walk progressing? If you don't look just like Jesus, that means that work is still left undone. To that end, let's continue to engage in what he started.

COMPILING THE PLAN

I believe you have truly wanted to grow in the past. Whether out of sincere desire or legitimate frustration, something has caused you to realize the need for change. Waiting around for an organizational event to address a personal issue has gone on for too long. We have to remember to number our days (Ps. 90:12) in order to activate us for focusing on essential areas right now. For all the desire you have possessed to grow, you might have remained stuck because you had no clear plan.

Our discipleship crisis is not due to a lack of sincerity but due to an oversight in intentionality.

Your growth has often been based on another's emphasis rather than your design. Someone else determined the sermon series, Bible study, targeted event, or specific ministry. While God probably used all of those mediums, you still have pertinent issues that need to be addressed in particular areas. Most likely, some of your individualized areas of growth will never be included in a strategy designed for a large group of people. With your Distinctive Discipleship plan assembled, you can start making progress in those key areas.

As a way of reminder, the last few chapters contained a process to narrow down potential areas of need into a targeted strategy to implement. By using these six areas from Col. 1:27-29, you developed a clear and comprehensive guide. The categories are:

1. **Delight** - finding your necessary motive
2. **Disobedience** - confronting your sinful leanings
3. **Doctrine** - strengthening your uncertain beliefs
4. **Development** - cultivating your needed maturity
5. **Discipline** - training your soul's habits
6. **Dependence** - acknowledging your desperate need

In the following pages, I have provided some helpful resources and blank worksheets to keep tabs on your plan or on the plans of those you are personally discipling. As you finalize your guide, you will possess a specific strategy to direct your discipleship efforts for the next few months of your life. To utilize these six categories, create action steps to start making improvements. Adjust along the way as you see fit. After a time of completing one pass of a plan, you can reevaluate your spiritual condition and fill in differing items for each category. You can continue to use this guide to fill out new guides until Jesus comes back, or you finally go to see him. You will continue to see progress.

STARTING THE TASK

I will reiterate the importance of having a specific plan and the benefit of aligning yourself with an intentional relationship. This plan is good for an individual, better with a partner, but best with a mentor. If you have identified an accountability partner or dedicated mentor to help you during this process, I believe you will go further faster. In solitary, possessing a specific guide for growth is superior to hopeful happenstance. Yet if you have someone walking beside you or in front of you, I am confident your journey will experience greater longterm success.

If you are considering using this guide to disciple another person, I want to encourage you to go for it. Don't listen to any voices that tell you that further growth is required before you can make a disciple. If you have learned anything in your discipleship, you have something you could teach to another. If you have acquired any wisdom along the way, someone else will relish the opportunity to learn the truths you might have taken for granted.

> **Find someone who is eager and teach him or her everything you know about following Jesus.**

Before I ever had a framework to utilize, I haphazardly attempted to make disciples. In those days, I so wish I had possessed a guide that could have focused my efforts. While God used my early attempts, the process was a bit scattered.

When I was an upperclassman in college, a freshman asked me a question I had never heard before. "Would you disciple me?" While the request was straightforward enough, I had no paradigm to use because I had never personally experienced what he was asking me to provide. So what should you do when someone asks you to do something of which you have no idea how to accomplish? I can tell you what I did. I responded, "Let's meet for breakfast on Thursday."

While I didn't know everything, I knew that he wanted to grow, and, for some unknown reason to me, he entrusted me with such a sacred oversight. With no curriculum or strategy in place, I simply assessed where he was spiritually, and I tried to address the most needed areas for him at that point on his journey. He was stuck in some areas in which, thankfully, I had seen a decent improvement in my life. He was seeking answers with some topics, of which I had never even considered the questions. He needed discernment regarding decisions that would impact his life. With each issue, we continually returned to studying Scripture, prioritizing prayer, and deepening dialogue.

At the end of our time in college, I honestly questioned how much help I had been to him. I was fully aware of my inadequacies, and I feared that the investment of my time was a total waste of his. In my thinking, he was going to contact me in a few years and tell me how his life had fallen apart, and how he held me responsible for my lack of direction in his life.

Over a decade later, he did reach out. He was traveling through town and wanted to get lunch. While I was excited to reconnect, I was honestly a little nervous about our interaction. Driving to meet him, I was preparing a legitimate alibi with which to defend myself. I had this fear that his marriage had failed, his doubts had resurfaced, or his growth had halted, and, somehow, I was responsible. After the obligatory introductory remarks, he got to the reason why he wanted to see me.

“I wanted to tell you that my family is going through a transition. Some recent developments have happened in my life, and I have to make some changes. In the coming months, we are moving overseas to be missionaries, and I can't thank you enough. I would never be going unless you had discipled me.”

When I say I was shocked, that is an understatement. Not only did I not anticipate his outlook, but it also made me question his recollection of our time together. If he thought I had made such an impact, had he even been paying attention? Apparently, he had. Despite my inexperience, my willingness to at least make an attempt made all the difference in the world. Well, it made all the difference in at least one country in the world.

God uses willing intentionality far more than seasoned capability.

Why would I tell you a testimony like that? If I were confident in my abilities, I would have told you that my stellar work in his life assured me of his success. Quite the opposite, I must admit. I am fairly confident that I felt unready, but I was willing. God used my incomplete efforts and is changing the world because of them. I have never been to my disciple's country, but part of me is there because I gave everything I had to him. As he goes, I go.

“You show that you are a letter from Christ delivered by us, written not with ink but with the Spirit of the living God, not on tablets of stone but on tablets of human hearts” (2 Cor. 3:3). On that mission field, he is my letter to a people I have never met. “Dear Friends, I don't know you, but you were so worth waking up for early on Thursday mornings while I was in college. I discipled your missionary so that he would share the gospel with you. While I didn't have the wisdom to see this plan, God did, and I am honored to play a small part in your story as well.”

That's how discipleship works. God uses our efforts and does more than what we could ever imagine. As you are discipled yourself and disciple others, you join in the glorious wonder that is the strategy of the Great Commission. Guided and empowered by the Holy Spirit, you can give yourself away to another. Through that relationship, God will impact nations yet unreached and generations yet unseen.

Your reading of this book bears witness to the fact that Jesus' plan is working. A Middle-Eastern carpenter assembled a ragtag group of followers and changed the world with them. As you read this book in a different language than what Jesus spoke, and in a different culture than where Jesus lived, something apparently worked and is still working. The baton passed from Jesus to Peter somehow made it to me, and I am trying to do my best to pass it on to you in some way. Centuries later, on the other side of the world, the goal to make disciples is still going strong, and we get to be a part.

God hasn't given up on you.

If you are alive to read this sentence, that means that he still has work left to do in you and through you. Join him in that process. Focus on the things that matter most. Make disciples.

Considering where you are right now and where you need to go, God has a specific set of charges designed just for you to get there. You don't need anyone else's directions, because they aren't in the same place as you. Your steps toward holiness will be as unique as you are.

Since every Christian is in a unique spiritual place with specific challenges, we know that a uniform template will not suffice for every single one of us. Instead of generalized approaches, I pray you would consider a Distinctive Discipleship strategy to narrow your focus, align your efforts, and implement your plan. We've made enough excuses; it's time now to make disciples.

RESOURCES

In the following pages, I have provided some resources to help narrow your focus to design a specific plan as well as some blank worksheets for a single guide or a group's list. You can use these guides to create your own guide, or you can use them to help another develop a plan as you disciple your mentee.

If you would rather not write your plan in the book, you can download numerous printable and digital worksheet formats at **travisagnew.org/distinctive**.

In addition to this resource, I developed ***The Distinctive Discipleship Bible Study***, which is an 8-week curriculum for a small group. This book or the Bible study workbook can operate independent of each other, or you can study through them at the same time to supplement the content. Within the workbook, I provided a guide to align what chapters to read at each week during the study.

Remember that the broad approach of this plan allows you to utilize it how it best fits your context. I pray the resources in the following pages and available online can help you further grasp this simple process and get going in the task of making disciples.

1. **Delight** - finding your necessary motive

   I need to delight in Jesus more than:

2. **Disobedience** - confronting your sinful leanings

   My disobedience that must be addressed is:

3. **Doctrine** - strengthening your uncertain beliefs

   The pivotal doctrine for me to study is:

4. **Development** - cultivating your needed maturity

   I need development in learning how to:

5. **Discipline** -training your soul's habits

   I will focus on the spiritual discipline of:

6. **Dependence** - acknowledging your desperate need

   My prayers of dependence will ask God to:

CATEGORY EXAMPLES

In case you struggle with selecting a focus for each category, here are some samples to acclimate your mind to the type of selection you need to make.

DELIGHT - I need to **delight** in Jesus more than:

- The approval of others
- My favorite technological device
- Staying busy for Jesus
- My favorite sports team
- My physical appearance
- My social media feedback
- My financial net worth
- My spouse's happiness
- Finding a spouse
- My home and possessions
- My children's success
- My favorite hobby

DISOBEDIENCE - My **disobedience** that must be addressed is:

- Alcoholism
- Crude joking
- Greed
- Fits of anger

- Pornography
- Sarcasm
- Refusing a Sabbath rest
- Racism
- Bitterness
- Flirtatious ways
- Consistent lying
- Stealing from work

DOCTRINE - The pivotal **doctrine** for me to study is:

- The Gospel
- The Biblical View of Marriage
- The Role of the Holy Spirit
- Predestination
- Old Testament Overview
- The Second Coming
- The Reality of Hell
- Image of God on Humans
- Deity of Christ
- Understanding the Trinity
- How the Bible is Really God's Word
- Gender Expectations in Scripture

DEVELOPMENT - I need **development** in learning how to:

- Share my faith
- Love my spouse
- Discern and use my spiritual gifts
- Address my finances
- Teach a Bible study
- Improve my time management
- Navigate through the Bible
- Disciple my children
- Be a better church member
- Improve my physical health for the glory of God
- Do my job more efficiently
- Show hospitality to my neighbors

DISCIPLINE - I will focus on the spiritual **discipline** of:

- Bible Reading
- Prayer
- Scripture Memory
- Fasting
- Worship
- Giving
- Sabbath rest
- Service
- Evangelism

- Church Involvement
- Solitude
- Journaling (Remembering God's faithfulness)

DEPENDENCE - My prayers of **dependence** will ask God to:

- Find peace from my past
- Calm my anxiety
- Reconcile my family
- Find a healthier work environment
- Save my friend
- Raise the money needed for missions
- Restore the joy of his salvation
- Make me patient
- Heal my neighbor's sickness
- Send more workers to the harvest
- Bring unity in our church
- Soften my spouse's heart

NAME:

BASED ON COLOSSIANS 1:27-29

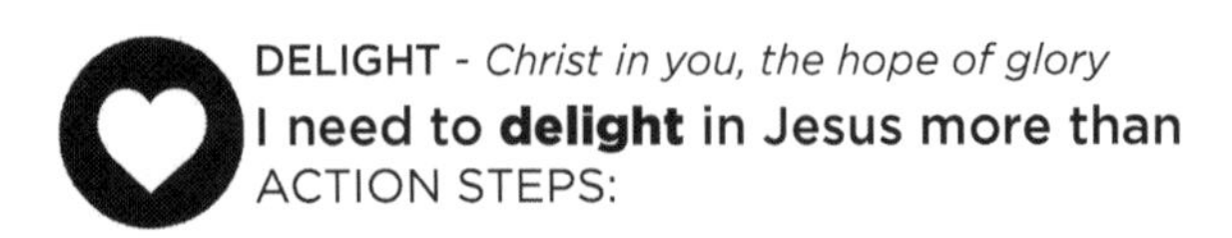

DELIGHT - *Christ in you, the hope of glory*

I need to **delight** in Jesus more than

ACTION STEPS:

DISOBEDIENCE - *warning everyone*

My **disobedience** that must be addressed is

ACTION STEPS:

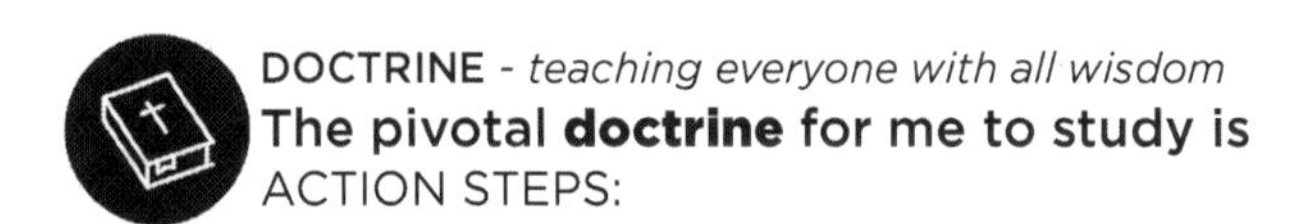

DOCTRINE - *teaching everyone with all wisdom*

The pivotal **doctrine** for me to study is

ACTION STEPS:

START DATE:

ESTIMATED END DATE:

DEVELOPMENT - *present everyone mature*

I need **development** in in learning how to

ACTION STEPS:

DISCIPLINE - *for this I toil*

I will focus on the spiritual **discipline** of

ACTION STEPS:

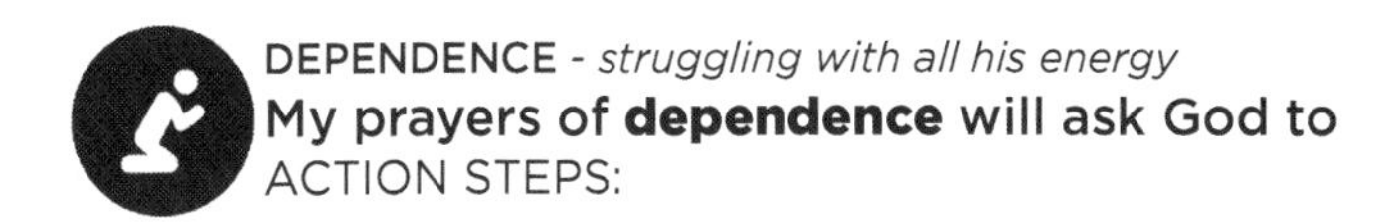

DEPENDENCE - *struggling with all his energy*

My prayers of **dependence** will ask God to

ACTION STEPS:

WHO WILL EVALUATE:

WHEN TO EVALUATE:

BASED ON COLOSSIANS 1:27-29

NAME:

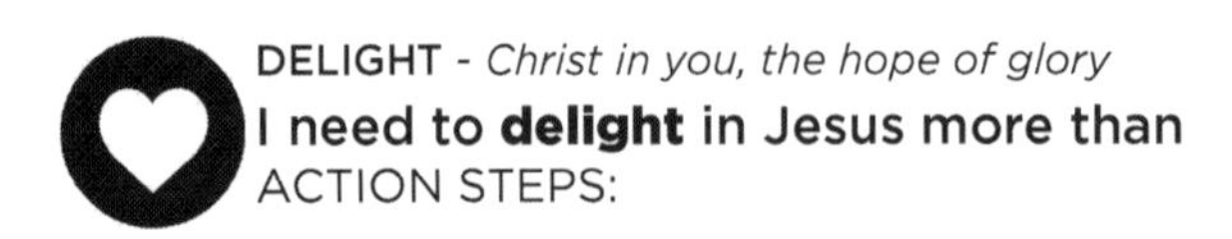

DELIGHT - *Christ in you, the hope of glory*

I need to **delight** in Jesus more than

ACTION STEPS:

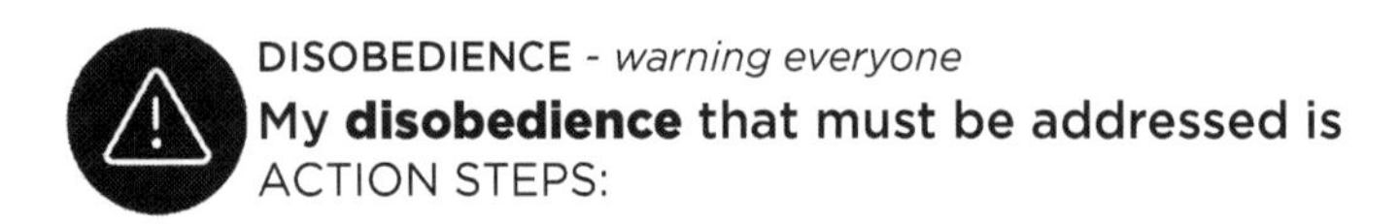

DISOBEDIENCE - *warning everyone*

My **disobedience** that must be addressed is

ACTION STEPS:

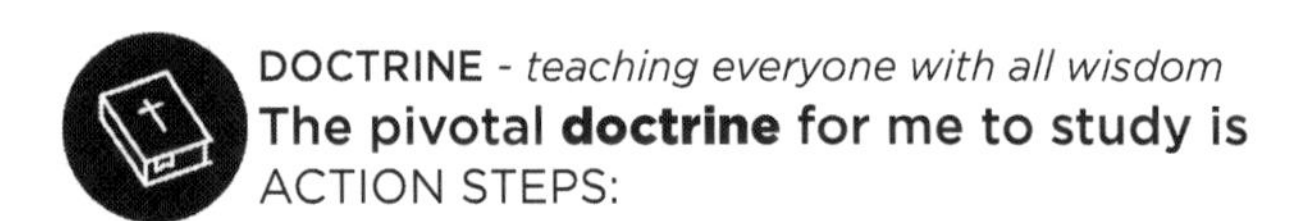

DOCTRINE - *teaching everyone with all wisdom*

The pivotal **doctrine** for me to study is

ACTION STEPS:

START DATE:

ESTIMATED END DATE:

DEVELOPMENT - *present everyone mature*

I need **development** in in learning how to

ACTION STEPS:

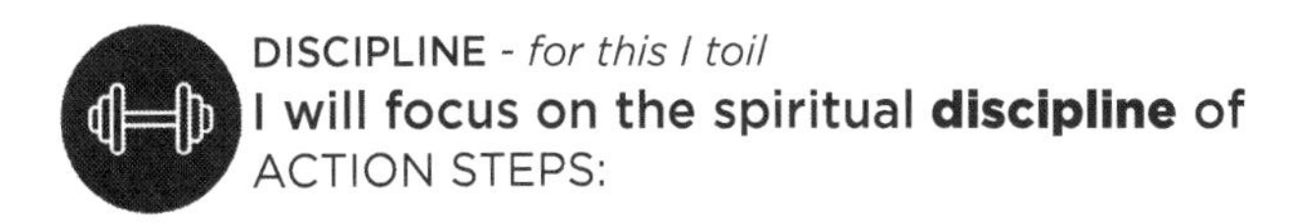

DISCIPLINE - *for this I toil*

I will focus on the spiritual **discipline** of

ACTION STEPS:

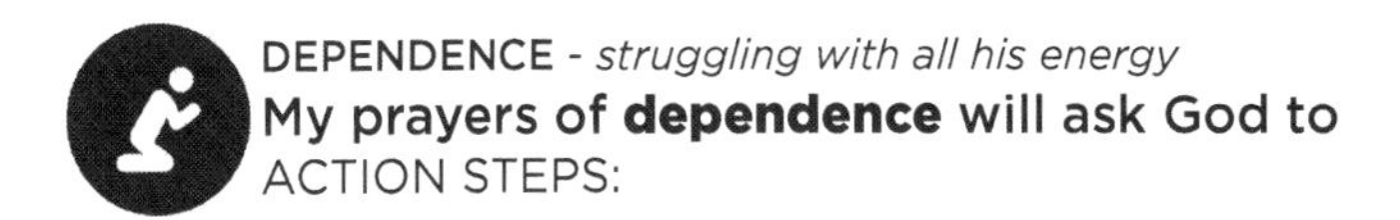

DEPENDENCE - *struggling with all his energy*

My prayers of **dependence** will ask God to

ACTION STEPS:

WHO WILL EVALUATE:

WHEN TO EVALUATE:

BASED ON COLOSSIANS 1:27-29

NAME:

DELIGHT - *Christ in you, the hope of glory*

I need to **delight** in Jesus more than

ACTION STEPS:

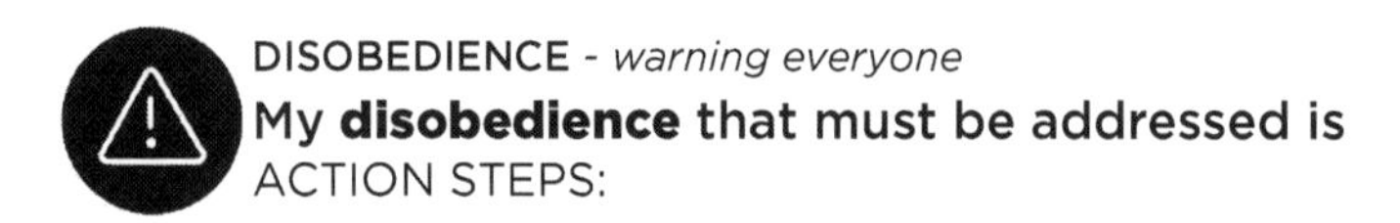

DISOBEDIENCE - *warning everyone*

My **disobedience** that must be addressed is

ACTION STEPS:

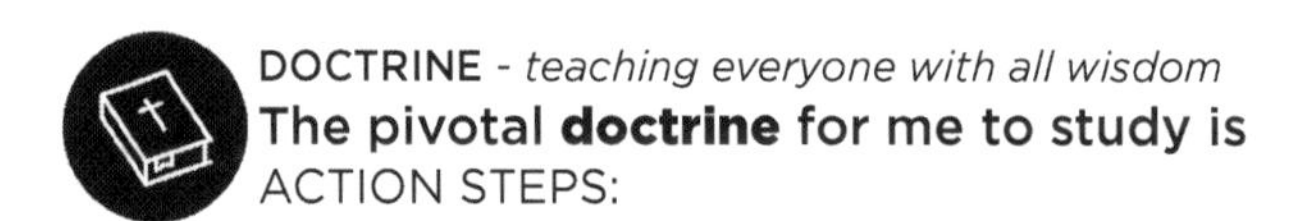

DOCTRINE - *teaching everyone with all wisdom*

The pivotal **doctrine** for me to study is

ACTION STEPS:

START DATE:

ESTIMATED END DATE:

DEVELOPMENT - *present everyone mature*

I need **development** in in learning how to

ACTION STEPS:

DISCIPLINE - *for this I toil*

I will focus on the spiritual **discipline** of

ACTION STEPS:

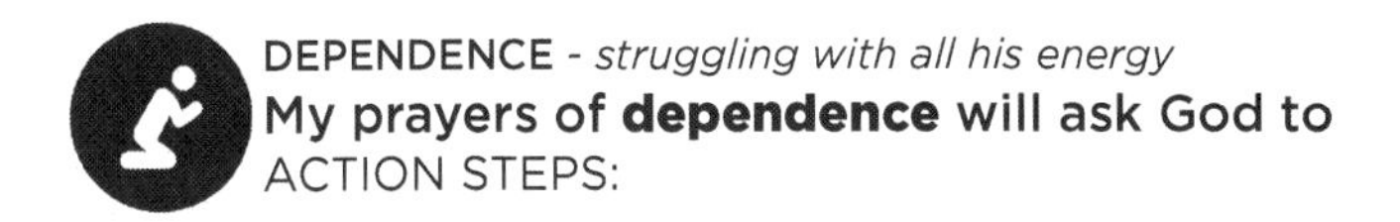

DEPENDENCE - *struggling with all his energy*

My prayers of **dependence** will ask God to

ACTION STEPS:

WHO WILL EVALUATE:

WHEN TO EVALUATE:

BASED ON COLOSSIANS 1:27-29

NAME:

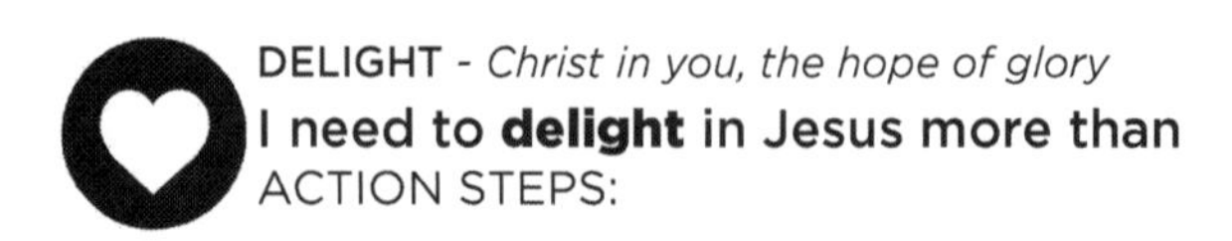

DELIGHT - *Christ in you, the hope of glory*

I need to **delight** in Jesus more than

ACTION STEPS:

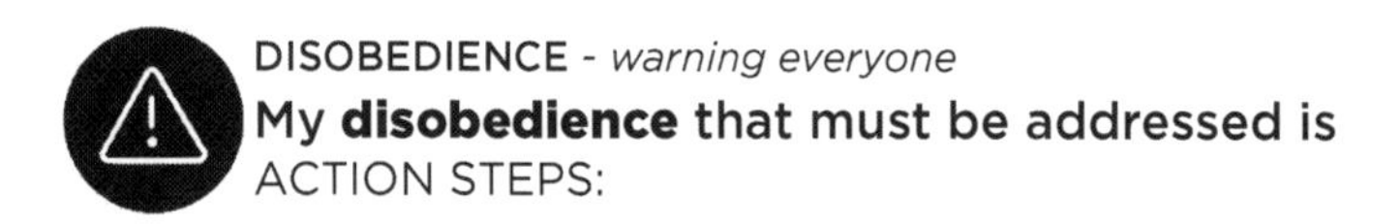

DISOBEDIENCE - *warning everyone*

My **disobedience** that must be addressed is

ACTION STEPS:

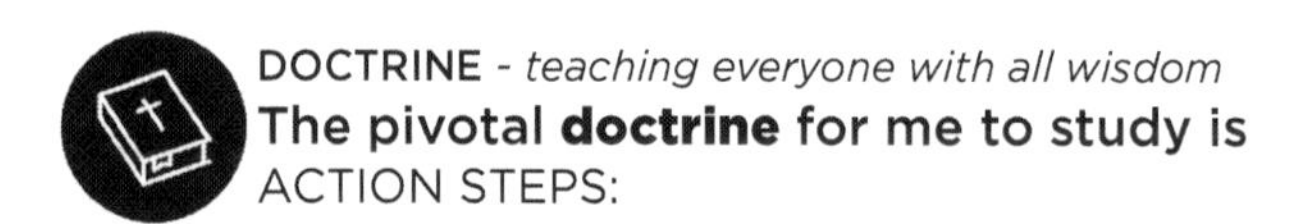

DOCTRINE - *teaching everyone with all wisdom*

The pivotal **doctrine** for me to study is

ACTION STEPS:

START DATE:

ESTIMATED END DATE:

DEVELOPMENT - *present everyone mature*

I need **development** in in learning how to

ACTION STEPS:

DISCIPLINE - *for this I toil*

I will focus on the spiritual **discipline** of

ACTION STEPS:

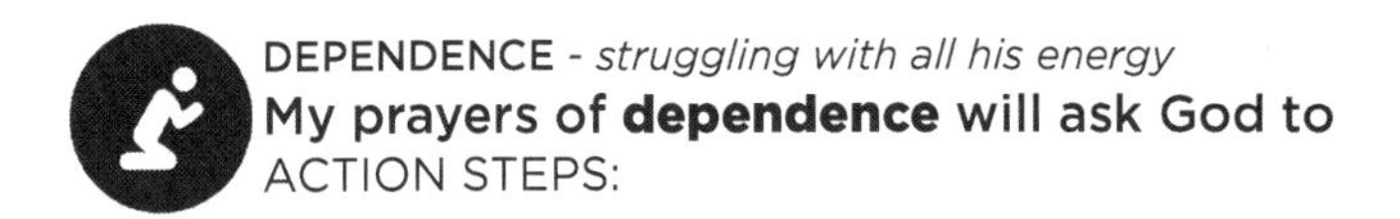

DEPENDENCE - *struggling with all his energy*

My prayers of **dependence** will ask God to

ACTION STEPS:

WHO WILL EVALUATE:

WHEN TO EVALUATE:

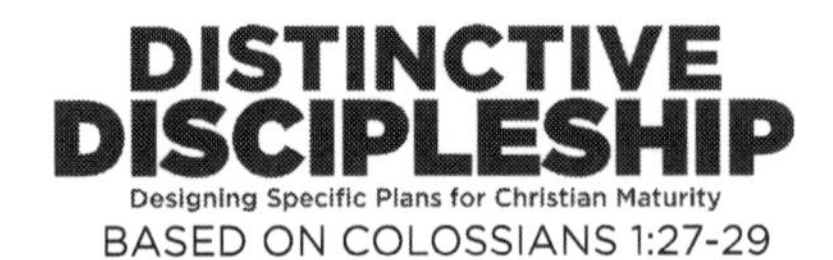

DISTINCTIVE DISCIPLESHIP

Designing Specific Plans for Christian Maturity

BASED ON COLOSSIANS 1:27-29

NAME:

DELIGHT - *Christ in you, the hope of glory*

I need to **delight** in Jesus more than

ACTION STEPS:

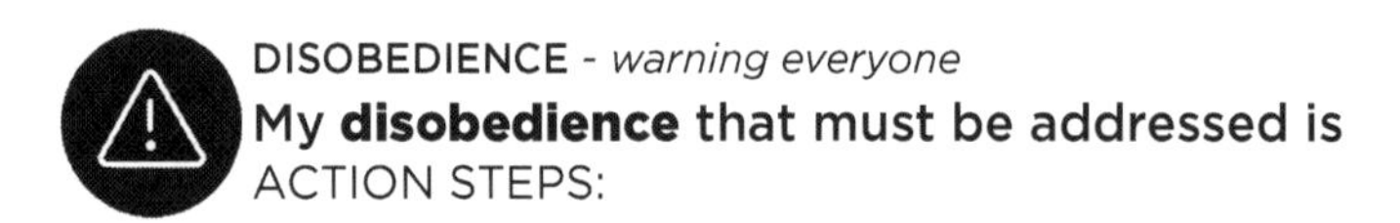

DISOBEDIENCE - *warning everyone*

My **disobedience** that must be addressed is

ACTION STEPS:

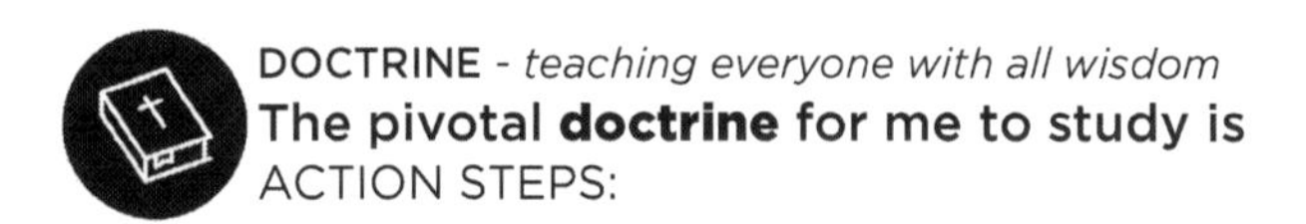

DOCTRINE - *teaching everyone with all wisdom*

The pivotal **doctrine** for me to study is

ACTION STEPS:

START DATE:

ESTIMATED END DATE:

DEVELOPMENT - *present everyone mature*

I need **development** in in learning how to

ACTION STEPS:

DISCIPLINE - *for this I toil*

I will focus on the spiritual **discipline** of

ACTION STEPS:

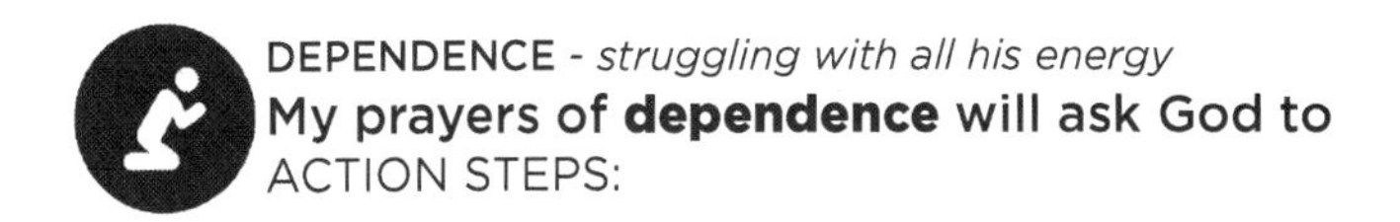

DEPENDENCE - *struggling with all his energy*

My prayers of **dependence** will ask God to

ACTION STEPS:

WHO WILL EVALUATE:

WHEN TO EVALUATE:

GROUP GUIDE

NAME:

 DELIGHT
 DISOBEDIENCE
 DOCTRINE

 DEVELOPMENT
 DISCIPLINE
 DEPENDENCE

NAME:

 DELIGHT
 DISOBEDIENCE
 DOCTRINE

DEVELOPMENT
 DISCIPLINE
 DEPENDENCE

NAME:

 DELIGHT
 DISOBEDIENCE
 DOCTRINE

 DEVELOPMENT
 DISCIPLINE
 DEPENDENCE

NAME:

 DELIGHT
 DISOBEDIENCE
 DOCTRINE

 DEVELOPMENT
 DISCIPLINE
 DEPENDENCE

NAME:

 DELIGHT
 DISOBEDIENCE
 DOCTRINE

 DEVELOPMENT
 DISCIPLINE
 DEPENDENCE

NAME:

 DELIGHT
 DISOBEDIENCE
 DOCTRINE

 DEVELOPMENT
 DISCIPLINE
 DEPENDENCE

NAME:

 DELIGHT
 DISOBEDIENCE
 DOCTRINE

 DEVELOPMENT
 DISCIPLINE
 DEPENDENCE

GROUP GUIDE

NAME:

 DELIGHT  DISOBEDIENCE  DOCTRINE

 DEVELOPMENT  DISCIPLINE  DEPENDENCE

NAME:

 DELIGHT  DISOBEDIENCE  DOCTRINE

 DEVELOPMENT  DISCIPLINE  DEPENDENCE

NAME:

 DELIGHT  DISOBEDIENCE  DOCTRINE

 DEVELOPMENT  DISCIPLINE  DEPENDENCE

NAME:

DELIGHT DISOBEDIENCE DOCTRINE

 DEVELOPMENT  DISCIPLINE  DEPENDENCE

NAME:

 DELIGHT  DISOBEDIENCE  DOCTRINE

 DEVELOPMENT  DISCIPLINE  DEPENDENCE

NAME:

 DELIGHT  DISOBEDIENCE  DOCTRINE

  DEVELOPMENT DISCIPLINE  DEPENDENCE

NAME:

 DELIGHT  DISOBEDIENCE  DOCTRINE

DEVELOPMENT DISCIPLINE DEPENDENCE

For more books, sermons, posts,
articles, and resources, visit

TRAVISAGNEW.ORG